DATE DUE

HOW A

CHANGED

For information about permission to reproduce selections from this book, please contact permissions@highlights.com.

Calkins Creek

An Imprint of Highlights

815 Church Street

Honesdale, Pennsylvania 18431

Printed in China

ISBN: 978-1-59078-732-8

Library of Congress Control Number: 2013953464

First edition

10 9 8 7 6 5 4 3 2 1

Designed by Robbin Gourley

Production by Margaret Mosomillo

Titles set in Sabotage Regular

Text set in Bodoni Std Roman

ACKNOWLEDGMENTS

I'm grateful for the generous help of those who shared their
knowledge and expertise with me. Thanks to Dr. Margaret
Humphreys, Department of History, Duke University;
Dr. Alan M. Kraut, Department of History, American University;
Dr. Virginia Utermohlen, Division of Nutritional Sciences, Cornell
University; Dr. Elizabeth Brake, Fuqua School of Business, Duke
University; Libby Marks, Department of Psychology, University of
Washington; the staff of the Wilson Special Collections Library,
the University of North Carolina at Chapel Hill; and the staff of the
Waring Historical Library, the Medical University of South Carolina.
For assistance with translations, thank you to Judy Goldman,
Lauren Worsham Jarrow, and Anna Marks.

I appreciate the talented team at Calkins Creek and Boyds
Mills Press who worked on this book, particularly Robbin Gourley,
who designed a visually dramatic *Red Madness*; Joan Hyman,
whose meticulous attention to detail always improves my work;
and Bonnie McCormick, who patiently assisted me with the book's
images. I'm especially grateful to editor Carolyn P. Yoder for her
wise suggestions, well-timed encouragements, and overall good
judgment.

Contents

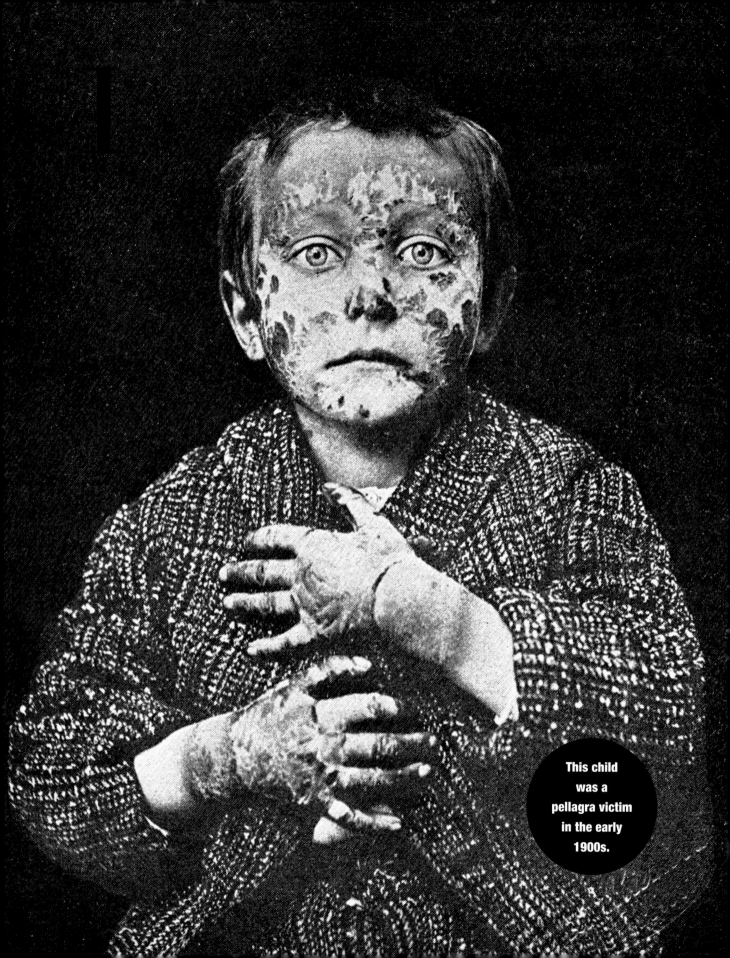

This child was a pellagra victim in the early 1900s.

GLOVE, BOOT, NECKLACE, AND BUTTERFLY

"An Awful and Loathsome Disease . . ."
—New York Times

Georgia, March 1902

The sandy-haired farm worker was desperate. His legs were so weak that he couldn't work. His skin burned. His stomach ached. Food tasted too salty. When he tried to eat, he vomited. He had a constant thirst, and no amount of water quenched it.

It wasn't the first time the twenty-nine-year-old had suffered this way. Every January or February since the age of fourteen, he had felt sick. In early spring, when he began working in the fields, his hands and the tops of his feet became bright red—much redder than a sunburn—followed by blisters and crusty scabs. He bounced back by the end of the summer, regaining his strength and the weight he had lost. But by the next February, the illness returned even worse than the year before.

This attack was unbearable. The previous spring, he had lost thirty pounds, about a quarter of his normal weight. He still hadn't gained back most of it, and now he was sick again. He would rather die than live like this. Hoping that a city doctor could finally help him after fifteen years of misery, the farm worker traveled to nearby Atlanta.

Dr. H. F. Harris was shocked when the young man described his problems and took off his shirt for the exam. The patient had the symptoms of pellagra, a dreaded disease in southern Europe. Harris had never seen a case before. American medical textbooks—if they mentioned pellagra at all—said that the disease wasn't found in the United States. Yet this man had lived his entire life in Georgia.

When Dr. Harris checked the most recent medical books, he learned that pellagra was a type of food poisoning from corn. After corn was harvested in the fall and stored through the winter months, it could spoil and become poisonous.

The doctor asked his patient about the food he ate. The farm worker admitted that he had been poor since childhood and that corn bread had always been the main part of his diet.

Dr. Harris advised his patient to avoid bread made from moldy corn. But he did not share his true fears with the young man. Harris knew of no cure for someone who had been sick with pellagra this many years. Eventually, the disease would take the young man's life.

One of pellagra's symptoms is a rash that breaks out on both the left and right sides of the body, starting out red and then darkening. This man has the rash on his neck, back, and elbows.

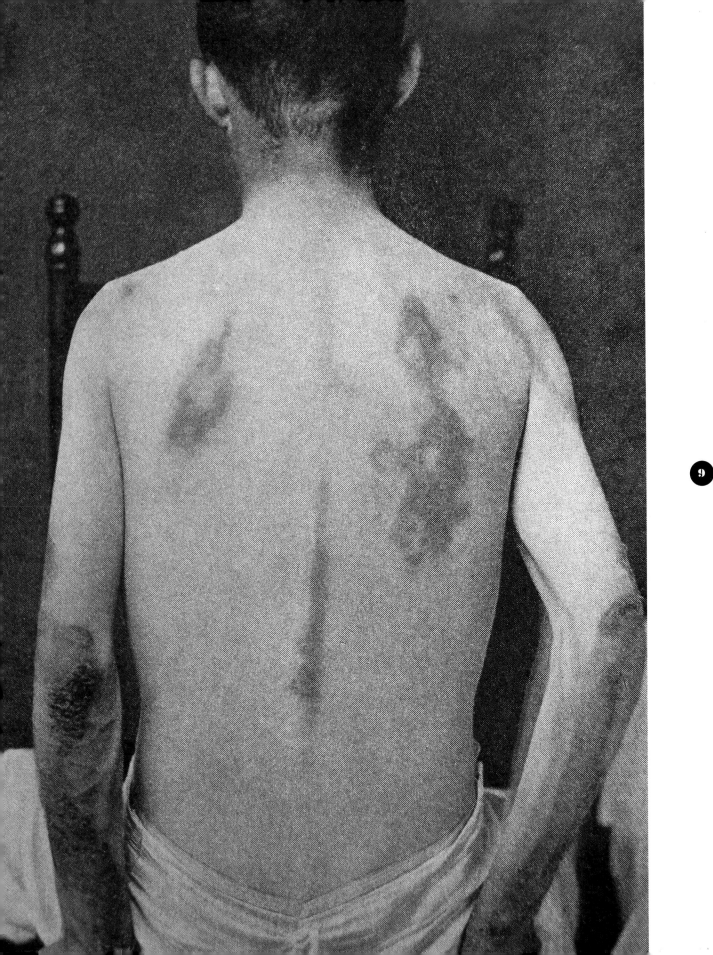

9

A month later, at a Georgia Medical Association meeting, Harris told fellow physicians about the farm worker. Other than those at the conference, however, few people heard about the unusual case of pellagra in America.

SOUTH CAROLINA, AUGUST 1906

The three children had played at the mill since they were old enough to go to work with their father. It was fun to eat a bit of fresh cornmeal while it was still hot from the grinding.

In the spring of 1897, the oldest—a five-year-old girl—developed diarrhea and a red rash on her hands and feet that lasted through the summer. A year later, she had the same ailments, and so did her four-year-old brother. When their little brother turned two in 1900, he also developed the illness.

Each spring, the attacks struck them with more intensity. Their parents thought that the children's yearly rash was poison ivy. They weren't particularly concerned about the diarrhea because the three children recovered by winter.

During the spring of 1905, when the older brother was eleven, he became so ill that he was too feeble to walk. He lay in bed for four months with severe diarrhea and vomiting, gradually wasting away. He died that August.

The next spring, his fourteen-year-old sister felt dizzy, staggering when she walked. In addition to the skin and sintestinal problems she'd had for nine springs, her stomach burned and her neck ached. She was so exhausted and frail that she couldn't get out of bed. By August 1906, she was dead.

Her eight-year-old brother, the youngest of the three children, was the only one left. His skin was red and peeling, he had mild diarrhea, and he couldn't stop drooling. But so far, pellagra had not killed him.

The pellagra rash on this boy's hands looks like gloves. It forms a butterfly shape across his cheeks.

An Alabama Epidemic, Fall 1906

The superintendent at Mount Vernon Insane Hospital was troubled. His patients were dying at an alarming rate.

Located in a small town thirty miles from Mobile, Alabama, the state-run hospital treated mentally ill black patients. Every summer since Mount Vernon had opened five years earlier, three or four patients developed a mysterious fatal ailment with identical symptoms. The superintendent assumed these deaths were due to the patients' generally fragile health.

But in the summer of 1906, 80 women and 8 men came down with the same disease. Most had been in the hospital for more than a year and had been fairly healthy until stricken that

The Mount Vernon Insane Hospital, where an epidemic broke out in 1906. At that time, institutions for the mentally ill were called insane or lunatic hospitals, asylums, or sanitariums. Today they are called psychiatric hospitals.

summer. Of the sick, 57 died, most within two or three weeks of showing signs of illness.

The superintendent knew he had an epidemic on his hands. He asked his son, Dr. George Searcy, to investigate. The young doctor had experience with epidemics. He had served in the tropical Panama Canal Zone, where mosquitoes spread deadly yellow fever and malaria to workers building the canal.

Dr. Searcy examined the remaining sick patients. Their hands and wrists were red and blistery. About a third of them had a rash on the back of the neck and top of the feet. A few patients had redness across their cheeks that looked like a butterfly lying on the face. Besides the rashes, many complained of stomach and intestinal upsets. Because nurses were not ill, Searcy concluded that the sickness wasn't contagious.

That Corn Disease

Based on what he'd seen, he was convinced that he was dealing with pellagra. Searcy was stunned to find an epidemic of the disease in the United States, where it wasn't even supposed to exist.

His medical books said that eating spoiled corn caused pellagra, so he compared the diets of the hospital's patients and nurses. He found that the patients ate corn bread and grits. Nurses ate a more varied diet that included white bread and biscuits.

The doctor decided to stop feeding corn products to the patients. Instead, he put wheat bread and potatoes on their menu. To make sure that corn truly was the key to the illness, Searcy left eight patients on their previous corn diet.

According to medical books in the early 1900s, corn and its products could cause pellagra.

After ten days, only a single new pellagra case developed. It was one of the eight patients still eating cornmeal. The health of the other seven in the corn group had deteriorated, too. Searcy stopped giving them corn and put the eight on the same non-corn diet that the other patients were getting.

He ordered the hospital's cornmeal analyzed to see if it was spoiled. As he suspected, the cornmeal was moldy and contaminated with bacteria and fungi—a food "unfit for human use."

Doctors, Beware!

George Searcy believed he had discovered the cause of the hospital's epidemic. In July 1907, he published an article in a national medical journal warning fellow doctors to be on the alert for pellagra, "especially in the south, where corn bread and grits are so largely used."

American doctors hadn't been trained to recognize pellagra. As they read Searcy's article detailing the symptoms, some of them remembered earlier illnesses that they weren't able to diagnose or cure.

At a hospital for the insane in Illinois, officials reconsidered a situation from the year before. The bodies of two dead patients had suspicious red marks. Nurses were accused of scalding them to death with hot bath water. Although the nurses denied it, they were fired. Now realizing that the marks had been signs of pellagra, hospital officials rehired the nurses.

One South Carolina doctor thought that he had seen cases among insane patients at his asylum as far back as the 1870s. Another doctor claimed that during the Civil War, more than forty years earlier, he had observed pellagra among Union soldiers held in the Confederate prisoner-of-war camp at Andersonville, Georgia. He recalled that the prisoners' diet had been limited to musty corn.

South Carolina, July 1908

Like many of her neighbors, the twenty-four-year-old mother of two young children worked in the cotton mill. Every spring for the previous ten years, she had developed diarrhea that lasted for several months. Although her bowel problems disappeared by winter, they came back the next spring.

As the diarrhea started up in the spring of 1905, the normally pale skin on her hands and arms became bright red. The woman felt depressed and nervous while she had the red rash, though the symptoms went away during the winter. The next year, her rash and diarrhea returned. Then tragedy struck—her new baby died. Her usual spring despair was even worse, and after two years, she still had not emerged from her depression.

In July 1908, the young mother began insisting that she could see and talk to her dead father. And every few hours, she grabbed her throat, crying that something inside it was burning. Her hands had to be tied down so that she didn't choke herself.

Doctors diagnosed pellagra, but it was too late. Within days, the woman was delirious, talking nonstop. Two weeks after her hallucinations had started, she died.

. . . she grabbed her throat, crying that something inside it was burning.

Workers tend the machines at a cotton mill in Newberry, South Carolina, in 1908. Women put in long hours at the mills and then went home to care for their children.

What the Italians Knew, Summer 1908

Dr. James Babcock was the fifty-two-year-old superintendent of the State Hospital for the Insane in Columbia, South Carolina. When the Harvard-educated physician read George Searcy's article about pellagra, he was worried. Babcock feared that the same disease had sickened patients at his hospital and likely would again. He wanted to learn as much as he could about it.

In the summer of 1908, Babcock traveled to Europe, where pellagra had been a plague for two hundred years. Hundreds of thousands of people—mostly poor rural peasants—became ill as the disease spread across Spain, France, Italy, and Romania and into Turkey and Egypt.

Babcock visited an Italian hospital where he saw pellagra patients. He confirmed that the terrible disease in South Carolina was indeed pellagra. He heard from Italian doctors that pellagra affected three parts of the body: the skin, the digestive system, and the nervous system. Depending on the person, the disease could strike one, two, or all of these body systems.

The symptoms usually appeared in the spring and disappeared with autumn's colder weather. Some pellagrins, as the Italians called afflicted people, were sick for many years. Others died within a few weeks of first showing symptoms.

The skin rashes created the telltale mark of pellagra. They appeared in places exposed to sunlight, most commonly on both hands, like a pair of gloves; on the feet, like matching boots; around the neck and down the chest, like a necklace; and across the cheeks, in a butterfly shape.

James Babcock (1856–1922) was born in South Carolina and graduated from Harvard University Medical School. After seeing many pellagra cases among patients in insane hospitals, Babcock dedicated himself to studying the disease and educating others about it.

The reddened skin became dry and scaly and then peeled. Some patients developed oozing blisters, scabs, and crusts. The rash cleared up during the winter months, although eventually the skin in the affected areas became rough, thick, and darker.

Pellagrins also suffered from stomach pain, nausea, vomiting, and foul-smelling diarrhea. Sometimes they produced so much saliva that they drooled and had to spit out the excess every few minutes. The tongue and mouth burned, and eating felt like "swallowing live coals."

Patients grew depressed, confused, and anxious. In the most serious cases, they had hallucinations and even tried to kill themselves. Insanity was usually soon followed by death.

Babcock realized that pellagra wasn't easy to diagnose. Its symptoms varied among people and were similar to other diseases. Skin rashes resembled sunburn, severely dry skin, and even leprosy. The debilitating diarrhea, occurring as often as twenty times a day, could also be caused by dysentery and intestinal parasites. Weakness and fatigue were symptoms of many illnesses.

An Egyptian peasant in the early 1900s has the dark pellagra rash on his lower arms and chest. The distinctive neck and chest rash is called Casál's Necklace, named after the Spanish doctor who first described it in 1735.

The Italians blamed pellagra on poisons in moldy corn. The reason the disease struck peasants instead of other people, the doctors told Babcock, was because corn was the only food the poor could afford. If that corn was spoiled, they ate it anyway . . . or starved.

When James Babcock returned to the United States, he was determined to raise awareness of the horrific disease. He spoke to medical groups, wrote articles, and gave newspaper interviews about pellagra and his trip to Europe. Physicians and pellagrins sought out his advice.

hen pellagra affected the brain, patients experienced depression, anxiety, confusion, and hallucinations. Some became suicidal. Today, we refer to a person with these conditions as having a "mental disorder." In the early 1900s, however, different terms were common and acceptable: *insane, mad, crazy, out of one's mind.* In keeping with the historical period, that language is used in this book.

South Carolina, October 1908

Anne Schumpert and her husband were well known in their small town near Columbia, South Carolina's capital. For some time, the elderly black woman had a strange rash. During a period of six months, she lost so much weight that she became emaciated. Then her mind slipped into insanity.

Two doctors were called to examine her, and they both diagnosed pellagra. They immediately sent her to the Hospital for the Insane in Columbia, where Dr. Babcock could treat her. The local newspaper reported on her condition. It stated that Anne had been "a very large eater of corn bread" and likely developed pellagra because the corn was "defective."

The News Spreads

Frightening headlines started to appear regularly throughout the United States: "Pellagra Found In This State," "South Menaced By 'Pellagra,'" "Dying Of A Rare Disease." Yet pellagra was still a mystery to most American doctors.

In Washington, D.C., Surgeon General Walter Wyman knew he had to do something about it. As head of the United States Public Health and Marine Hospital Service, Dr. Wyman

17

or more than two hundred years, the United States Public Health Service has helped to control disease and protect health and safety.

The Service got its start in 1798 when the U.S. Congress established marine hospitals to care for sick seamen. In the 1870s, the Marine Hospital Service began to focus on the control of contagious diseases such as smallpox, cholera, and yellow fever. The Service established its Hygienic Laboratory in 1887 to study diseases and their causes. The Laboratory was an early step in the federal government's funding of disease research, carried out today by the National Institutes of Health.

In the early 1890s, the Service was charged with keeping infectious diseases out of the country through the examination of immigrants and the quarantine of ships. Its medical officers traveled wherever epidemics broke out. They had the authority to quarantine people in order to control a disease's spread.

In 1902, its name changed to the U.S. Public Health and Marine Hospital Service. Ten years later, it became the Public Health Service, the name used today. The PHS is part of the Department of Health and Human Services.

Walter Wyman (1848–1911) was born and raised in St. Louis, Missouri, where he earned his medical degree. Wyman joined the U.S. Marine Hospital Service in 1876 and became surgeon general in 1891, a post he held for twenty years.

was responsible for the nation's health. He suspected that many people had pellagra, but their doctors didn't recognize what was wrong with them.

In 1908, Surgeon General Wyman assigned Dr. Claude Lavinder, one of the Service's young researchers, to study pellagra. He wanted Lavinder to find out what caused the disease, how it was transmitted to humans, and how it could be controlled.

Because so little had been published in English about pellagra, Wyman ordered a report detailing what was currently known from the Europeans. He then sent the information to health officials in each state, urging them to count their cases.

News of pellagra victims came in from hospitals for the insane, orphanages, and private physicians. By the summer of 1909, the Service recorded at least 1,500 cases that had occurred in the Southern states since 1906.

South Carolina was at the top of the list with 500 cases. Georgia and Alabama each had about 200, and North Carolina reported 75. The Service began including a count of pellagra victims in its weekly bulletins just as it did for the deadly diseases smallpox, bubonic plague, tuberculosis, and typhoid fever.

More cases appeared every week. "The disease has arisen and grown to large proportions," observed Lavinder, "apparently like the proverbial mushroom, almost in a single night."

Pellagra was spreading. But no one was sure why, or how it could be stopped. America's new deadly disease was on the way to becoming a national epidemic.

Claude Lavinder (1872–1950), originally from Lynchburg, Virginia, investigated pellagra for the Public Health Service during the early years of the epidemic.

19

n 1735, Gaspar Casál, a doctor in northern Spain, wrote about a sickness he considered the most disgusting he ever encountered. He had seen it among peasants, who called the disease *mal de la rosa* ("illness of the rose") because of its red rash.

About forty years later, Francesco Frapolli described the same disease among peasants in northern Italy. Unaware of the Spanish *mal de la rosa*, the Italian doctor wrote that the ailment was "not only very severe and very prevalent but generally unrecognized." The Italian peasants, who had definitely recognized the disease, called it *pellagra* ("rough skin").

Soon pellagra was identified in France and Romania. It afflicted hundreds of thousands of Europeans during the eighteenth and nineteenth centuries. Doctors who studied it agreed that the victims were almost always peasant farmers. But they did not agree on pellagra's cause.

A few doctors claimed it ran in families and was hereditary. Some connected it to the peasants' wretched poverty, which caused them to live in unsanitary homes and to eat only poor-quality vegetables. Noticing that the red rash appeared on exposed skin, other doctors blamed the sun's strong spring and summer rays.

When pellagrins ended up in a hospital, doctors could only treat their symptoms. They didn't know how to cure the disease. The most common treatments for skin rashes were warm and cold baths and drugs that caused sweating. For stomach pain, vomiting, and diarrhea, doctors gave patients tonics and wine. To build up a pellagrin's strength, hospitals served nourishing foods, including meat. Some patients received an arsenic mixture, which doctors believed brought improvement.

By the middle of the nineteenth century, European pellagra experts concluded that eating something harmful caused the disease.

They narrowed it down to corn, the main food of most pellagrins. In fact, in Italy the *only* food many peasants ate was polenta, a mixture of ground cornmeal and water.

The experts thought that pellagra cases did not occur in a region until corn became a staple food there. History seemed to support their theory. As far as anyone could tell, pellagra had not existed in Europe before explorers brought corn to Spain from America in the late 1400s. Because corn was easy to grow and produced an abundant and tasty food, it became a popular crop in southern Europe.

What was it about corn that led to this ghastly disease? Nineteenth-century doctors noticed that pellagra symptoms appeared in the spring when peasants were eating the last bits of corn left over from the previous season. Since corn became moldy after many months of storage, doctors reasoned that an unknown poison in the spoiled corn caused pellagra.

To avoid this, the French government encouraged its people to grow potatoes and grains other than corn as their main crop. By 1900, pellagra had nearly disappeared in France.

In 1902, the Italian government passed a law to stop citizens from eating spoiled corn. Farmers were warned not to harvest corn that was wet or still unripe, conditions that led to mold during storage. No one was allowed to sell moldy corn or anything made from it. Communities had to report pellagra cases to the government and provide pellagrins with unspoiled corn so that they could recover. Despite this, as many as 50,000 Italians suffered from pellagra in 1908, with new cases appearing every year.

k written
Casál
1762. It shows
e pellagra rash:
the top of the
around the neck.

2

In this 1909 photograph, the pellagrin's melancholy expression suggests that his brain has been affected. Pellagra is called the 4-D disease because its symptoms are dermatitis (rash), diarrhea, dementia (mental disorder), and death.

BAFFLED BY PELLAGRA

"The more you study pellagra, the less you think you really know about it."
—*Dr. James Babcock*

In October 1909, Miss Sue Woods died miserably in a North Carolina hospital. Her death made the front page of newspapers across the nation, from Pennsylvania to Florida and from Virginia to Missouri. But it wasn't just because the thirty-year-old woman was the daughter of a Mississippi

Supreme Court justice—a "prominent girl," as a Georgia headline called her. It was because she died of "that rare disease which is baffling the physicians of this country." During the three weeks Sue suffered in the hospital before her death, doctors from miles away came to study her and learn about "the strange malady."

Pellagra had seized the attention of the public and confounded doctors. What caused it? Why were people suddenly dying from it?

The answers from Europe didn't satisfy alarmed Americans. There, pellagra was a disease of peasants. Everyone believed that in the United States, even poor people lived much better than Italian peasants. Besides, prominent citizens like Miss Sue Woods were dying of pellagra, too.

A Virginia boy (left) stands in the middle of his family's cornfield in the early 1900s. By 1909, many Southern farmers had switched from growing corn to cotton. Some of the bolls, the golfball-sized capsules on this cotton plant (right), have split open, revealing the fluffy cotton fibers. At a cotton mill, the fibers were spun into thread, which was woven into cloth.

If corn caused the disease, why hadn't pellagra shown up before? Americans had always eaten corn. Corn bread and grits were important parts of the Southern diet.

It was true that farmers in the South planted less corn than they once had, because cotton brought more money. As a result, Southerners were eating more corn grown in the Midwest and buying products like cornmeal made in other states. Were these products causing pellagra? And what about the hundreds of cases reported in the North?

A Scourge

In November 1909, more than three hundred physicians, scientists, and public health officials met to discuss these questions. The group held their conference at the State Hospital for the Insane in Columbia, South Carolina, where Dr. James Babcock was superintendent. They called themselves the National Association for the Study of Pellagra. There was no time to lose. "We are menaced with a national scourge," warned one doctor.

The U.S. Public Health and Marine Hospital Service sent an assistant surgeon general to speak to the group. He announced that the number of reported pellagra cases had more than tripled to 5,000 during the previous four months. This was partly because physicians had become more aware of the disease.

Trying to calm fears that pellagra was contagious, he told the group that the Service had no reason to believe pellagra spread directly from person to person. The Europeans had long experience with the disease, and they didn't quarantine their pellagra patients. But to be cautious, the Service's officers in Italy were not allowing anyone with signs of pellagra to immigrate to the United States.

Although a strong connection between pellagra and corn seemed to exist, the federal government didn't recommend that people stop eating the grain. Without doubt, corn was a nutritious food. Until more was known, the safe approach was to avoid eating *moldy* or *spoiled* corn.

Physicians at the conference showed revealing photographs of their tormented pellagra patients. For many in the audience, it was their first look at the appalling disease.

Some speakers shared the cures and remedies they used, including tonics made from arsenic and strychnine, powerful chemicals that were thought to cure a range of illnesses. A few doctors recommended opium to reduce diarrhea and nitroglycerine for skin rashes.

Other physicians vehemently disagreed with these remedies. "I have had extensive experience with this disease," insisted one South Carolina doctor, "and I have seen no drug that would cure it."

A second doctor added that none of the medicines had any benefit and, in fact, made the patient sicker. His patients did best when he took them off corn and gave them meats, fresh vegetables, and fruits.

In the Dark

Everyone had the same question: What causes pellagra?

Most of the world's experts connected pellagra to decomposing corn. They believed that a bacterium or fungus grew on spoiled corn, and that was what sickened people.

Several speakers at the conference supported the moldy corn theory. According to them, their patients improved during the late summer months because they were eating fresh vegetables and fruits without mold.

One physician blamed the pellagra outbreak on new farm machinery.

This eleven-year-old North Carolina girl has the pellagra rash on her lower arms and face. She died just four months after her rash first appeared in the early 1900s. Her younger sister also developed pellagra but recovered.

26

When the machinery gathered cornstalks into tight bundles, it allowed a fungus to grow. He predicted an increase in pellagra after a wet season. Another doctor countered by saying that in Italy and Egypt, pellagra was worse after a drought and food shortages.

Not everyone in the audience was persuaded by the corn theory. So far, no pellagra-causing microorganism or poisonous chemical had been discovered. Some doctors reported that they saw pellagra patients who *never* ate corn products. Besides, they said, it was hard to prove if a pellagrin had eaten spoiled corn. How could anyone know whether the cornmeal they bought was made from bad corn?

A woman collects corncobs in a field. At the 1909 pellagra conference in South Carolina, one doctor claimed that bundling the stalks allowed a pellagra-causing fungus to grow on the kernels.

A British scientist had a completely different idea. He proposed that a small blood-sucking blackfly infected humans with a pellagra parasite in the same way that mosquitoes caused malaria and yellow fever. The scientist hadn't yet identified the parasite. But he pointed out that pellagra symptoms appeared in the spring when the biting blackflies emerged. He claimed that pellagrins often lived or worked near water where the flies bred.

By the end of two days, nobody at the conference had been able to definitely explain what caused pellagra. The audience applauded in agreement when a Florida doctor said: "If there is any one thing that this conference has forced upon me, it is the belief that we do not know the [cause] of pellagra; that we are today in the dark."

North Carolina, Fall 1909

The woman was forty-one, but to the doctor she looked at least twenty years older. She told him that she had five children, ages fourteen years to fifteen months. She had never been sick before her vexing troubles had started six years earlier. That was the first spring she developed diarrhea and stomach pains. The debilitating symptoms came back every spring and summer. In the fifth spring, she noticed a bright red rash.

Now, in the sixth year, she'd been sick for three months. The backs of her hands were peeling. Her body was stinging, and her legs and feet felt as if they were on fire. Her mouth tasted salty. She hadn't been able to sleep, and her memory was failing. The distraught woman admitted that she'd had hallucinations.

Three weeks later, the doctor saw her again. Her family told him that she refused to stay inside the house. She called her children foul names, and they had become afraid of her.

Not long after the doctor examined her, the crazed woman grabbed an ax and wandered around her yard looking for a person she declared she had to kill. The family's only choice was to commit her to the insane hospital before she hurt someone. No one could help her now. Within a few weeks, the woman was dead.

. . . the crazed woman grabbed an ax . . .

28

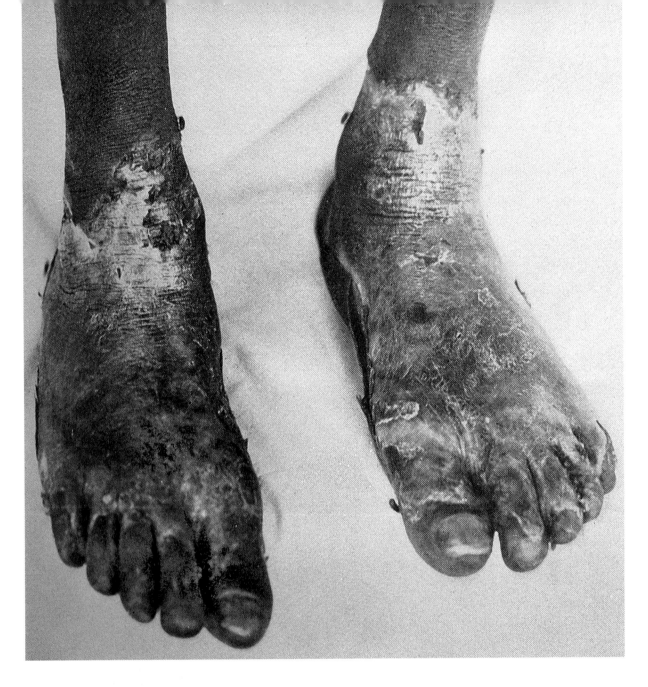

The Deadly Poison

The continuous stream of chilling newspaper stories
about pellagra made the public more anxious. An article in the
Biloxi Daily Herald described the ghastly death of a Mississippi
woman: "It attacked the mucous membrane of the mouth,
throat and stomach and finally affected the brain."

A Kentucky newspaper used graphic language to inform
its readers: "There is a new disease pellagra which comes from

**The pellagra rash on feet
looks like boots.**

eating corn affected by mold. This mold is the deadly poison that kills its victims by slow degrees and in greatest agony. It tortures the skin, undermines the strength, weakens the mind, converts its victim into a gibbering idiot and finally brings death."

An article in a Pennsylvania newspaper described a Louisiana woman and her five children who all suffered from "Incurable Pellagra." The caption under their photograph explained why: "Musty cornmeal gave dread disease to this family."

Many people stopped eating corn after they read the *New York Times* headline "If You Fear Pellagra Beware of Corn."

But some Southerners were unwilling to go that far. A North Carolina columnist wrote: "We of the South can not and do not wish to give up corn bread[,] hominy grits, fritters and all the other good, nourishing and strengthening products on which we have grown and thriven."

Corn lovers embraced any news that took the blame off their favorite food.

Virginia, August 1910

According to her family, fifty-five-year-old Mrs. A. Sallie Graham of Warrenton, Virginia, *never* ate corn. Her health had been good until she developed a skin irritation that wouldn't go away even with the creams and medicines her doctor gave her.

After six months, she began to forget things and wondered if she might be going insane. When her family told the doctor that Sallie's mind was slipping, he reassured them that she was just run down.

Soon Sallie fell into a coma. Her family took her to a Washington hospital fifty miles away. The doctors there immediately diagnosed what her hometown doctor had missed—pellagra.

After six months, she began to forget things . . .

DIES OF PELLAGRA

Mrs. A. Sallie Graham Expires in Georgetown Hospital.

FIRST VICTIM IN CAPITAL

Patient, in Coma for Two Weeks, Baffles Skill of Doctors.

For ten days, they tried to revive Sallie, but she never regained consciousness. The news of her death appeared on the front page of the *Washington Post*. She was the first pellagra fatality in the nation's capital.

Headline from the August 30, 1910, edition of the *Washington Post.*

Pellagra Madness

As repulsive as the skin rashes and diarrhea were, pellagra's most dreaded symptom was insanity. European

This despondent woman died ten days after the photograph was taken in the early 1900s. Once the disease affected their brains, pellagrins often died within a short time.

32

experts estimated that as many as 10 percent of pellagrins lost their mind.

One woman under treatment for the disease wrote her doctor: "I have fought this madness each minute, saying I would not go insane. . . . My brain would grow so dark that I forgot god and family, forgot everything save this awful despair."

Pellagra victims often felt confused and afraid. When one ailing woman was brought to the hospital, she cried, "I'm scared, I'm scared. What are you going to do to me? Am I going to be killed?"

Many patients had terrifying hallucinations. An agitated woman told nurses that bugs and snakes were crawling around her hospital room at night. Others imagined wicked ghosts hovering around them, or their bodies being hanged, or their children tortured.

Doctors were seeing more and more patients in this advanced stage of pellagra. Many of these people hadn't sought medical help until they'd experienced symptoms for several years. They began to crowd the Southern insane asylums, where pellagra became the number one cause of death.

Nine years had passed since Georgia's Dr. H. F. Harris reported the first case of pellagra in the United States. Yet the medical community had failed to find a way to save people before they descended into insanity and death.

Mississippi, April 1911

Mrs. Dora Roberts came from a well-known and respected family in southern Mississippi. When her doctor told her that she had pellagra, she was devastated. She feared what would happen next. The symptoms would worsen, and they would be horrible. She had no hope of recovery. Dora waited until her family left the house. She went into the privy and—as the local newspaper put it—"blew her brains out."

The symptoms would worsen, and they would be horrible.

n the years following the Civil War, the South struggled to recover from its defeat. Cotton was its biggest and best crop, and Southern leaders and businessmen built factories to turn that cotton into cloth.

By the 1880s, Southern cotton mill owners were successfully competing with the textile mills in the North. They saved money on shipping raw cotton to the mills because it grew in the nearby fields. They had a cheap source of labor— poor white farmers eager to leave the land for a mill job. The mills hired few black workers.

Even though these former farmers earned less than Northern mill workers, they were glad for the steady wages in the cotton mills. They no longer had to worry about a failed crop putting them into debt. Mill work was easier, too. On a farm, chores never ended.

Entire families had jobs in the mills, including children as young as eight. Some states set limits on child labor, but the laws were routinely broken. With two parents and several children working at the mill, families earned more money than they could as small farmers.

Mill owners built plain, wood-framed houses near the mill and rented them to their workers. Villages sprang up, particularly in North and South Carolina, Georgia, and Alabama. The mill owners usually ran a company store from which workers bought their food and other household goods. It was often the only store in town.

Every day a whistle echoed through the village, calling people to the mill. Workers were on the job for ten or eleven hours a day for five days a week, plus five hours on Saturdays.

3...

This man has a pellagra rash around his ear and on the side of his head.

TACKLING THE MYSTERY

"In the history of medicine the profession has been led into many serious errors through deductions made from false observations."
—*Dr. Claude Lavinder*

Georgia, Summer 1914

The fifty-year-old farmer knew he had pellagra because his parents had it, too. After three years of attacks, his health declined rapidly. By the time he was brought to the hospital, he was emaciated and confused. His tongue was cracked and beet red, and he could barely speak. The skin on his hands and up to the elbows was peeling. His face and ears were rough and scaly. When the man tried to walk, he staggered and fell.

The hospital's doctors put him in bed and attempted to build up his strength. They fed him four times a day with meats, dairy products, salads, and vegetables. For medicine, they gave him quinine, strychnine, arsenic, and iron mixtures. After a month of this treatment, the farmer was stronger. His mind was still not clear, but the doctors were confident that he would continue to improve.

"A National Calamity"

By fall of 1911, the Public Health Service (PHS) had collected reports of pellagra cases in forty states. At least 30,000 people had come down with the disease since 1907, most in the Southeast and Gulf states. One newspaper reported that almost every doctor in South Carolina had at least one pellagra patient in his practice.

A shocking number of them died. In eight Southern states (Alabama, Georgia, Kentucky, Louisiana, Mississippi, North Carolina, South Carolina, and Virginia), the disease killed an average of nearly 4 in 10 pellagrins—a total of more than 6,000 deaths. That did not include the insane asylums, where the death rate was as high as 6 in 10.

In November 1911, Surgeon General Walter Wyman died suddenly, and a new surgeon general took over. Dr. Rupert Blue, forty-four, had established his reputation by fighting bubonic plague and yellow fever epidemics. Blue had been raised in South Carolina, and he was just as concerned about the pellagra outbreak as Wyman had been.

Rupert Blue (1867–1948), the surgeon general from 1912 to 1920, was born in North Carolina and grew up in South Carolina. He joined the Marine Hospital Service in 1892 and worked there until he retired in 1932.

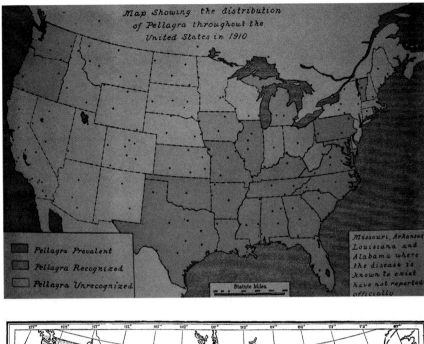

Map Showing the distribution of Pellagra throughout the United States in 1910

Pellagra Prevalent
Pellagra Recognized
Pellagra Unrecognized

Missouri, Arkansas Louisiana and Alabama where the disease is known to exist have not reported officially

Statute Miles

The top map shows where pellagra was reported in 1910, based on surveys of state officials. Data for the bottom map, published in 1912, came from state boards of health, private physicians, and heads of public institutions, such as insane asylums.

The differences between the two maps reflect the increased reporting as more doctors and state officials learned about the disease. Some of the Northern states that seemed to have many pellagra cases in 1910, such as Pennsylvania and Illinois, were adjusted by 1912 to show these cases in isolated pockets, mainly in insane asylums.

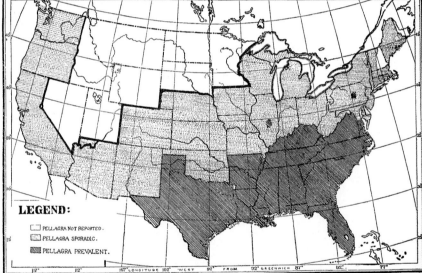

LEGEND:
PELLAGRA NOT REPORTED.
PELLAGRA SPORADIC.
PELLAGRA PREVALENT.

In his annual report to the U.S. Congress for 1912, Blue wrote: "In many sections of the country the disease now prevails in epidemic form and is menacing the life and health of the entire population." He called pellagra "a national calamity."

Two PHS researchers were busy studying it. Dr. Claude Lavinder, who had spent the previous four years working on the epidemic, examined pellagra patients at the Service's marine hospital in Savannah, Georgia. He also conducted laboratory experiments to find out how the disease was spread and how it could be treated.

During the summers of 1911 and 1912, Dr. R. M. Grimm traveled to communities in Georgia, Kentucky, and South Carolina, where pellagra was rampant. These areas included cotton mill villages, coal mining camps, and farms.

Grimm talked to local doctors and visited their patients, counting how many people had pellagra and recording where they lived. He asked pellagrins when they first developed symptoms and whether any relatives had had the disease. He found out what they ate and where they obtained food and drinking water.

Thanks to Grimm's detailed investigation, a picture of America's pellagra epidemic emerged. He found that the disease was more common in small towns and villages than in cities. It usually sickened people between early spring and late summer, then disappeared during fall and early winter.

Of the 1,400 cases that Grimm investigated, the majority of victims were younger than age fifty. More poor people had

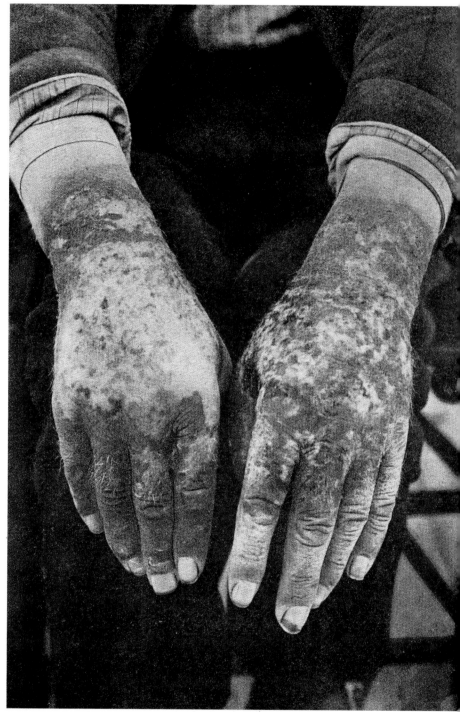

The rash on this South Carolina boy's hands has begun to peel.

pellagra than did wealthy ones, and more whites had it than blacks. Women of both races developed pellagra more often than men did.

The disease was fatal for 3 in 10 people, with blacks far more likely than whites to die. The average age of death was forty-three. Although many children developed pellagra, their cases tended to be milder, and they usually survived.

Grimm concluded that the epidemic was probably worse than the PHS realized. Doctors didn't report the cases because many pellagrins never sought medical care. "Pellagra," he wrote, "is more prevalent than is ordinarily supposed even by the physicians practicing in pellagrous communities."

Oklahoma, August 1911

Eight-year-old Esther Duff was the daughter of Chief Henry Duff of the Creek Nation. According to news accounts, she was "the richest Indian child in the world." Her father had become a multimillionaire after oil was discovered on his family's land. When Esther fell ill with pellagra, he promised a fortune to the doctor who cured her. Many tried, but all failed. The doctors told Esther's parents that her disease was in its last stages and she was beyond help. Even her father's wealth could not prevent Esther's death.

Investigation in Illinois

The Public Health Service wasn't the only group trying to solve the pellagra mystery. In Illinois, 500 people—most in insane asylums—were diagnosed with the disease from 1909 to 1911. The governor appointed a commission of doctors and scientists to investigate.

At the end of 1911, the commission's final report rejected the corn theory, saying it didn't matter whether people ate too much corn or none at all. Furthermore, spoiled corn had not

When Esther fell ill with pellagra, [her father] promised a fortune to the doctor who cured her.

11

caused the Illinois pellagra cases. The corn eaten by insane patients was in perfect condition, as one would expect in the nation's top corn-growing state.

The commission believed that a pellagra-causing microorganism infected the human body, possibly in the intestines. The idea that illness could be caused by microorganisms—the germ theory—was proved during the second half of the nineteenth century. By 1911, scientists and doctors had identified several diseases caused by microbes, including tuberculosis, malaria, and typhoid fever, and they were looking for more.

But the Illinois commission couldn't find a pellagra microbe or parasite in patients, and the group wasn't sure how the organism entered the body. The scientists tried to infect monkeys and other animals using body fluids and feces of pellagrins. Yet the animals didn't develop pellagra.

The report noted that when two of the state's mental asylums served more meat to their patients, the pellagra cases decreased. A third asylum reduced the meat portions, and its pellagra rates went up. The commission speculated that a diet low in animal protein "may so alter the body that the infecting organism has a better chance to grow."

Investigation in South Carolina

At about the same time, two wealthy philanthropists concerned about the spread of pellagra donated $15,000 to investigate the disease. Colonel Robert M. Thompson, of New York City, was a former navy officer who served as president of the American Olympic Committee in 1912. J. H. McFadden, from Philadelphia, was known for his donations to hospitals and medical research. Both men were involved in businesses that bought and sold cotton.

The Thompson-McFadden Pellagra Commission included doctors and medical researchers. During 1912 and 1913, they studied every known case of pellagra in Spartanburg County, South Carolina.

The county had more than two dozen cotton mills, each with its own village for workers and their families. Nearly a quarter of the county's 83,000 people lived in these villages. The rest lived in city or rural areas. Local doctors, mill owners, and residents cooperated with the investigation.

The researchers examined each pellagrin's health history, diet, housing, work, family, and lifestyle. They were looking for conditions that pellagrins shared with each other but that were different from healthy people. In the laboratory, other researchers analyzed the pellagrins' stomach juices, blood, feces, and urine.

The Commission learned that cotton mill villages had the most pellagra cases. Housewives between ages twenty and forty-four were victims of pellagra more than people of any other age. These women accounted for four times more cases than men.

Like the Illinois Pellagra Commission, the Thompson-McFadden team saw no connection between the disease and what people ate. Pellagra wasn't caused by eating corn—either fresh or spoiled, too much or too little. Canned foods didn't bring on pellagra, and eating fresh meat and eggs didn't prevent it.

The researchers identified only one food that seemed to reduce the risk of getting the disease—milk. Pellagra was less

In 1912, two girls walk on a path near the Saxon Mill (on the right) in Spartanburg, South Carolina. Mill owners cooperated with the Thompson-McFadden Pellagra Commission study because they needed healthy and strong workers and were eager to learn what caused the disease.

common in families that kept a cow and drank milk daily. People who never used milk were more likely to have pellagra. Yet milk alone didn't prevent the disease; some people who drank it every day still became sick.

The Commission did not think pellagra was the result of a food missing from the diet. After all, they observed pellagra in "well-nourished growing children, . . . as well as in apparently well-nourished adults."

Above: Housewives with children were the most likely group to have pellagra, according to Thompson-McFadden researchers. In 1911, this Virginia mother posed on the porch of her run-down mill house. Her husband worked at the mill.

Left: The Commission found that families who owned a cow were less likely to develop pellagra. These children stand in front of their mill house in Chester, South Carolina, in 1908. The three boys worked in the Wylie Mill.

It's Catching

The Thompson-McFadden researchers found that people who lived with or next door to a pellagrin tended to get the disease. Even though several members of a family might have pellagra, there was no evidence that they inherited it. Instead, the Commission concluded that pellagra was a contagious intestinal infection.

What exactly caused the infection? The Commission didn't know. It could be a bacterium, as in typhoid fever, although laboratory researchers couldn't find it in the pellagrins' intestines or blood.

How did the infection spread? The group wasn't sure about that, either. Perhaps people passed it to each other through direct contact. Or maybe food was contaminated by sewage. Researchers saw more pellagra cases in mill villages where houses were close together and unsanitary outhouses allowed human waste to stay on top of the ground. The Commission suggested that communities could stop the spread of pellagra by disposing of human waste properly.

Another way the pellagra germ might be transmitted was by an insect. Entomologists studied insects in the Spartanburg area. Their investigation eliminated mosquitoes, fleas, lice, cockroaches, bedbugs, and the biting blackfly suspected by the British scientist. If an insect was the carrier, the entomologists considered the stable fly and housefly to be the best candidates.

The Thompson-McFadden Commission's researchers had conducted America's first thorough scientific study of pellagra. Many doctors took it seriously and accepted the conclusion that pellagra was an infectious disease.

Not So Fast . . .

But not everyone agreed. A Mississippi doctor claimed that *his* research revealed pellagra in homes where bedbugs and fleas were numerous. One of these insects, he said, carried a pellagra-causing parasite. He was working on identifying what it was.

An Alabama physician said that milk didn't *cure* pellagrins; it made them worse. When he eliminated milk from the diet, his patients improved.

One doctor in Kentucky believed that migrating birds like robins carried pellagra to the South. A Mississippi newspaper reported that a family caught pellagra from their cat.

Many mill villages were poorly kept, like this one at the Adelaide Mill in Anniston, Alabama. Houses were crowded together and sanitation was poor. In this 1914 photograph, the mill is in the background.

In Georgia, a doctor proposed that sugarcane, not an infection, was the cause. He noted that Southern mill workers and farmers, who suffered high rates of pellagra, were "extremely fond of all sugar-cane" products. According to him, a poisonous substance in sugar and syrups damaged the liver and intestines, leading to pellagra. When his patients stopped eating sweets, they improved or were cured. The reason pellagra had suddenly appeared in recent years, he explained, was because new methods of producing syrup concentrated the poisons. With the cost of syrup so low, poor Southerners were eating more of it.

Despite the range of explanations, most of the medical community believed that pellagra was the result of either infection or poisoning by spoiled corn. When the National Association for the Study of Pellagra met for its second meeting in October 1912, the group discussed both views.

Several researchers had looked for a pellagra microbe. They tested the blood, feces, and urine of live patients as well as the hearts, brains, and nerves of the dead. Nobody had been able to find a bacterium, parasite, or any other microorganism with a link to pellagra.

Two speakers talked about diseases that were caused by neither microbes nor poisons. Called deficiency diseases, these illnesses developed in people who ate a limited diet lacking in some essential substance. One example was scurvy, a disease common among sailors who ate no citrus fruits while they were at sea. Another was beriberi, seen in Asian countries among people who ate practically nothing but white rice without its natural brown skin.

These speakers mentioned a Polish biochemist named Casimir Funk, who had recently discovered the missing substance connected to beriberi. Funk thought that pellagra's symptoms were similar to beriberi. Because pellagra seemed to involve a diet limited mostly to corn, he suggested it might be another deficiency disease.

As the second pellagra conference drew to a close, the group was forced to admit that pellagra remained a mystery. Surgeon General Rupert Blue told the audience: "If the cause and nature of the disease were known, steps could be taken toward its cure and eradication; but, as a matter of fact, our knowledge of the disease today is almost as faulty as it was fifty years ago."

Georgia, November 1912

Mrs. John Parker, age thirty, was a grocer's wife. Her pellagra symptoms had advanced to insanity, and she twice tried to commit suicide. Her anxious family watched her closely, fearing that she might try again.

One morning she borrowed a knife, saying that she needed it to peel an orange. Instead, she slipped away to the outhouse and stabbed herself over and over in the chest until someone found her. Mrs. Parker did not survive.

People with beriberi may suffer weakness or paralysis in their legs, as well as fatigue and nerve or heart damage.

47

fter the South lost the Civil War, its agriculture system changed dramatically. Large-scale landowners needed a way to replace their slave labor, made unconstitutional by the Thirteenth Amendment in 1865. They set up a system in which they rented parcels of their land to individual farmers for growing crops. In much of the South, that crop was either tobacco or cotton.

A tenant farmer owned his mules and tools. He paid the landowner a set rate for use of the land. Tenants frequently needed an advance from the landowner in the spring to buy seeds, fertilizer, and other supplies. They paid off their debt after selling the crop at the end of the season.

Unlike a tenant farmer, a sharecropper borrowed a mule, tools, and supplies from the landowner. He paid for these and his rent with a share of the crop he grew, often half.

With the increase in textile mills in the South, the demand for cotton rose. Landowners required their tenants and sharecroppers to use as many acres as possible to grow it.

Because so much Southern farmland was devoted to cotton, the region did not produce enough vegetables and fresh meat for its people. These foods had to be shipped by railroad from other parts of the United States, which made them more expensive. Some fresh foods were too perishable to ship. Rural areas were isolated from the railroads, making many foods unavailable to the people living there.

Even farm families, who once provided their own food, no longer had room for a vegetable garden or animals. The cotton was planted right up to the porch of their wooden houses. They bought their food, instead, at a local store often run by the landowner. The stores stocked cornmeal, bacon, and molasses—foods the impoverished farmers could afford. When a farmer had no cash, he bought on credit.

The sharecroppers and tenant farmers lived year to year, adding to their debt in the spring and hoping to repay it in the fall. If the crop failed or selling prices tumbled, a farmer didn't earn enough to pay off his debts. He struggled to support his family, praying that next year's crop would be better.

4
...

This young
South Carolina man
has the pellagra rash
on his hands, elbows,
and face.

"The disease appears to spread, as if some agent of infection were everywhere."
—*Dr. Harrison Garman*

The germ theory was a recent idea in medicine, and doctors now knew that microbes caused epidemic diseases like typhoid fever and bubonic plague. It made sense to many of them that germs caused pellagra, too. Perhaps a pellagrin directly infected another person. Or maybe an insect host transmitted the pellagra microbe.

But how did the pellagra germ get to America in the first place? For some people, the logical answer was that recent immigrants had brought it.

From 1900 to 1910, nearly nine million immigrants entered the United States. The majority came from eastern and southern Europe where pellagra had been a longtime scourge. Two million came from one country—Italy. Most of them were poor and uneducated, and many Americans wished that they hadn't come. Didn't pellagra suddenly emerge in the United States after these people showed up?

Newspapers and magazines blamed the Italian immigrants, "who have been swarming into this country in such multitudes." The *Washington Post* connected pellagra's appearance in Mississippi farm areas to Italians who moved there: "There is a suggestion that pellagrous Italians may have migrated to this country." One magazine writer declared that sick immigrants infected a biting blackfly with the pellagra germ. The fly then bit and infected healthy Americans the way mosquitoes transmitted malaria.

When Mrs. John B. Connor died of pellagra in the Good Samaritan Hospital in Lexington, Kentucky, the newspaper headline read: "Wife of Railroad Foreman Believed to Have Caught Disease From Italians." The article stated that Mrs. Connor had done charity work among Italian railroad workers, who apparently infected her.

Italian immigrants line up in 1911 to be transported to the immigration station at Ellis Island from the ship that brought them to the United States. An immigration official oversees the process.

Who's at Risk?

If it was true that pellagra was a disease that people *caught*, some individuals seemed more likely to catch it. Government surveys revealed that vulnerable groups included alcoholics; women who were pregnant or had children; people who were dirty; and those infested with intestinal parasites such as hookworm, which was a widespread problem in the South.

Doctors speculated that these characteristics damaged health and made a person more at risk. The poor were especially weakened because they had insufficient food, lived in unclean surroundings, and often drank contaminated water.

Several researchers noticed that pellagra frequently ran in families, with two or three generations affected. They concluded that

Around 1912, three members of this Kentucky family have pellagra: the mother, the child sitting, and the one standing on the right.

pellagrins, particularly poor whites, had inherited a weakness that made them susceptible. Most American doctors didn't accept this idea, but a vocal group pushed their view.

One doctor in Atlanta, Georgia, argued that heredity protected certain groups. He claimed that Jews rarely developed pellagra, no matter where in the world they lived. This proved that they were immune to the disease because of their "inherited vitality."

Other researchers were puzzled by differences in pellagra rates between the races. In some places, more white people than black had it, even where blacks were the majority of the population. One researcher said that black people were less likely to be infected through contact with others because they lived on isolated farms. On the other hand, many whites with pellagra lived in crowded mill villages where germs could easily spread.

A Virginia doctor proposed two explanations for the racial differences. Black people were either less likely to go to a doctor when they developed pellagra, so their cases weren't counted, or they were less prone to the disease.

In other locations, the racial rates were reversed. One doctor declared that three-quarters of the cases in the South were black women. According to the health officer for Adair County in Kentucky, "It occurs more frequently among the colored, than the white people, because the colored citizens eat more corn-bread than do the whites."

"Grimm" Work

In 1913, the Public Health Service's Dr. Grimm reported on the pellagra cases he had surveyed in Southern communities. He wrote that in rural areas, nearly all of the pellagrins were impoverished tenant farmers or sharecroppers. Coal miners also had high rates of pellagra. Many of the pellagrins Grimm saw were cotton mill workers. He described them as "poor, overworked and underfed."

Mrs. Henry Lee, of McColl, South Carolina, was one of the cotton mill people. After her husband died, she went to work at the mill in order to support her three young children. Her wages were meager, and her life was miserable. A year later, she died of pellagra. Her three children were sent to an orphanage.

Grimm observed that people in cotton mill villages and the coal mining camps "lived out of paper sacks." They bought almost all of their food—dried and canned—in the company store, instead of growing vegetables or raising animals like cows or chickens. In the rural areas, very few of the tenant and sharecropper families had vegetable gardens or livestock. Most depended on a local store with its sparse food choices.

Based on what he'd seen, Grimm concluded that "the relationship between food and pellagra seems to be a real one." But he didn't have enough information to say how—or which—foods brought it on.

Southern doctors challenged Grimm's suggestion that pellagra in the South was connected to the lower economic classes. The chairman of the Pellagra Commission for North Carolina wrote: "The disease is not confined to the poorer element of our population. I have seen pellagra in society women, in teachers, in professional men, in bankers, in wealthy merchants."

Mills provided work for widows with children, but the wages often weren't enough to support a family.

Texas, Summer 1913

Ila Howard was a widow with five children . . . and pellagra. Because she was destitute, the county and the local relief organization took care of her family. When Ila's health deteriorated, she was hospitalized. No one expected her to recover.

The county probation officer went to her house to gather her children and transport them to an orphanage. The oldest, a fifteen-year-old girl, refused to go. She fought so fiercely that two sheriffs had to force her into the car.

After one night at the orphanage, the five children were sent to their grandparents two hundred miles away. The headline of the newspaper article about the family read: "Pellagra Robs Five Children of Mother."

Coal miners work by candlelight in 1906. They had to buy most of their food from a company store in the mining camp, where the choices were limited.

Don't Kiss a Pellagrin

So far, scientists hadn't found a poison, germ, or parasite that caused pellagra. Several researchers tried to infect test animals—and even humans—with materials from pellagrins' bodies. But they never succeeded in bringing on the disease. Apparently, pellagra wasn't easy to transmit from one person to another.

A doctor who treated children at two South Carolina orphanages noted that pellagra didn't spread nearly as easily as measles and whooping cough. More than 90 percent of the orphans caught those diseases, but only about 10 percent developed pellagra.

Yet others warned that pellagra was *extremely* contagious. A professor of dermatology at Vanderbilt University in Tennessee recommended that "a patient suffering from pellagra should . . . be quarantined or separated from close association with other members of the family, and . . . the room, bedclothing, and vessels should be disinfected."

Another physician cautioned: "Owing to the possibility of pellagra being infectious, we consider that such close contact as kissing of pellagrins should be avoided." Some Southern hospitals refused to admit pellagrins, they said, "because the disease is contagious."

Newspapers ran headlines like "Beware of Pellagra," adding to the public's distress. Although no one had proved that pellagra was contagious, the *fear* of catching the disease was spreading. It was called pellagraphobia.

When a Florida woman traveled to Georgia to see a doctor who specialized in pellagra, someone at her hotel found out that she had the disease and told the other guests. They forced the hotel's owner to kick her out.

After a woman in Georgia developed pellagra, her friends shunned her and her family came to visit only when absolutely necessary. Families even tried to hide that a loved one was a pellagrin. This made the plight of the victims more tragic.

Along with pellagraphobia came the shame of having a disease associated with poor, dirty people. One Kentucky health officer informed citizens "it is a disease that abounds in filth." A Georgia woman was so embarrassed by her pellagra diagnosis that she begged her doctor not to tell her son.

Some people believed that such a vile disease must be a punishment from God. One despairing man pleaded with his doctor: "Please tell me whether committing sin or moral wrong will bring on pellagra. Somehow my affliction appears to be of Divine infliction."

Doctor's Orders

According to doctors' reports throughout the South, 10 to 60 percent of pellagra victims died. Pellagrins in mental asylums had the highest rate of death, in part because they were already in the last stage of the disease—insanity— when admitted.

Physicians tried their best to help patients. But many thought that all they could do was to bolster a patient's strength to fight off the disease. That meant rest and a nutritious diet—without corn, just in case that was pellagra's cause.

Pellagrins with intestinal problems usually were able to digest eggs, buttermilk, oatmeal, and potatoes, and their health often improved on such a diet. Some doctors believed this confirmed that corn was to blame. One declared that people in the South had "corn-bread poison."

Because pellagra seemed to be a disease of warm temperatures, physicians told patients to travel to cooler places, such as the mountains or northern states. One doctor pushed for artificially refrigerating insane asylums. Since the sun brought out the skin rash, doctors warned patients to stay in the shade or indoors.

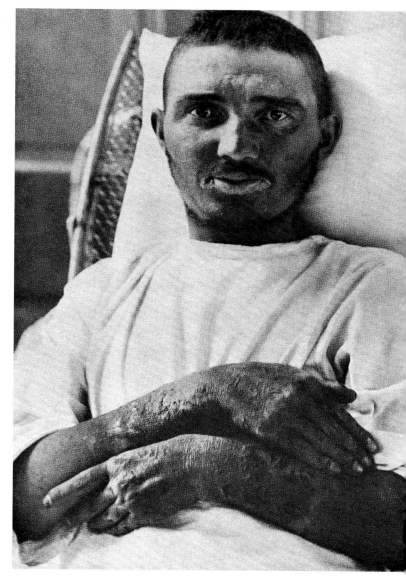

This South Carolina pellagrin's hands, face, and lips are covered with the rash. His vacant look is a sign that his mind is also affected.

Other physicians used more aggressive treatments. Ignoring studies that showed no benefit from medicines, they swore by injections of arsenic-based drugs. They were certain that the drugs destroyed infectious microbes or counteracted pellagra poisons.

Dr. A. D. Cudd, the director of a South Carolina hospital, claimed that he successfully treated pellagra by removing the end of a patient's appendix. This opened a pathway to the large intestine, which he flushed with antiseptic solution. His treatment worked, Cudd said, because the lower intestine was the home of the pellagra germ.

In three of his four cases, the patients recovered. The fourth patient died three days after the operation, Cudd explained, only because she had an advanced case of pellagra. He boasted to a gathering of doctors that his method was "the best treatment for pellagra known at present."

A Texas doctor reported that he healed patients with his town's mineral water, which purged the pellagra poison from the body.

A Florida physician announced that he cured pellagra with electricity. He ran an electric current between the patient's head and feet for thirty minutes twice a day. His patients recovered nicely, he said.

The Blood Treatments

Another new pellagra treatment involved blood transfusions to replenish the patient's weakened blood with that of a healthy person. When a Texas woman became frail and emaciated from the ravages of pellagra, her doctors decided to try it. They asked for volunteers to donate blood.

William Conti, a two-hundred-pound bookkeeper, was chosen from among the volunteers. One of his wrists was bound to one of the woman's. The doctor cut a blood vessel in each wrist, which he joined and held tightly together for thirty minutes. After an hour, the woman's breathing was less labored. Color returned to her cheeks. Later, she was able to eat, and Mr. Conti was hailed as a hero.

A Tennessee man's hands show the sharp line dividing normal skin from the pellagra rash, producing the appearance of gloves.

In Austin, Texas, sixteen-year-old Lulu Whitehead bravely donated a pint of her blood to save her mother from pellagra. A few months later, to treat its pellagra patients, a Texas sanitarium advertised for blood from "a young person, not addicted to intoxicants or tobacco."

Doctors tried blood transfusions of all kinds. Some thought that an unknown element in the blood of a recovered pellagrin could fight the infection in a sick patient. One researcher claimed success after transferring blood serum to a pellagrin from a horse with an ailment he considered similar to pellagra. A Romanian doctor gave his pellagra patients two dozen injections of radioactive blood serum to replace what he thought were the crucial missing elements in their blood.

These treatments often did not work, and the patient died. The proponents of the miracle cure explained the death by saying the patient was too far gone for *any* remedy to work. When a person recovered, it wasn't clear which cure had actually helped, because doctors routinely used various treatments at the same time.

Georgia, Summer 1913

William Bettis's wife was suffering from pellagra. He tried to raise extra money to take care of her and buy her medicines, but he couldn't come up with enough. No longer able to bear the grief of watching her slow and agonizing death, William resolved to end his own life.

After his children were in bed, he swallowed a bottle of laudanum, an opium-based patent medicine. When he collapsed to the floor, his wife awoke and screamed. Other family members rushed into the room and then sent for an ambulance.

Doctors at the hospital were able to save William. When he regained consciousness, he realized that he was as much a failure at killing himself as he had been at helping his wife.

When he collapsed to the floor, his wife awoke and screamed.

Opium-based drugs like laudanum were sold without prescription in the early 1900s. This display shows patent medicines advertised to cure babies of colic, restlessness, constipation, worms, and teething.

Sure Cure

Many sick people lost confidence in their doctors' advice and treatments. Others couldn't afford to see a doctor. The public was looking for a sure cure for pellagra, and the sellers of quack medicines were ready to oblige.

Advertisements for "Dr." Baughn's remedy ran in Southern newspapers. They were written like regular news articles with headlines such as "Cured of Pellagra; Woman Is So Happy." The ads quoted letters signed by people from real towns, praising Baughn's Pellagra Remedy for healing them in two weeks.

The Baughn Remedy's makers sent a booklet, *Pellagra Cured!*, to communities like mill villages where pellagra was widespread. It described pellagra's symptoms, some of which were so general that they fit almost any ailment: "Have you pains and aches for which there seem no cause?" The booklet used frightening language about "the MAD HOUSE and DEATH." There was just one hope for the "grim specter, stalking unseen up and down the land, touching with the icy hand of death," and that was Baughn's Pellagra Remedy, available in capsules or powder. And it cost only $10.

The American Medical Association analyzed the "remedy" and found that its main ingredient was iron sulfate. This chemical was sometimes given to people with iron deficiency, although it hadn't been shown to provide any benefit to pellagrins. The remedy also contained charcoal, salt, dirt, and straw.

Another quack medicine, the EZ-X-BA Remedy, came in liquid and sugar-coated tablet form. Buyers didn't know that this "remedy" included chemicals that, besides offering no cure for pellagra, made their digestive symptoms worse. Directions in the package said: "Nausea and nervousness usually follow in five to fifteen days after the treatment has been started, but this is an indication that the remedy is getting in its work."

Desperate to be cured of their wretchedness, pellagra victims were willing to try anything. When nothing worked, they felt total hopelessness. One wrote: "On my darker days, my thoughts are pessimistic and it seems to me that my case cannot be cured. . . . I am thinking of the awful death ahead of me and the motherless children that I shall have to leave."

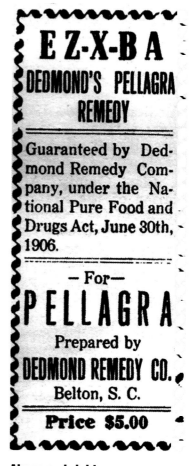

Above and right: These advertisements for pellagra remedies were reprinted by the *Journal of the American Medical Association* in March 1912 as part of an article exposing the contents of quack cures.

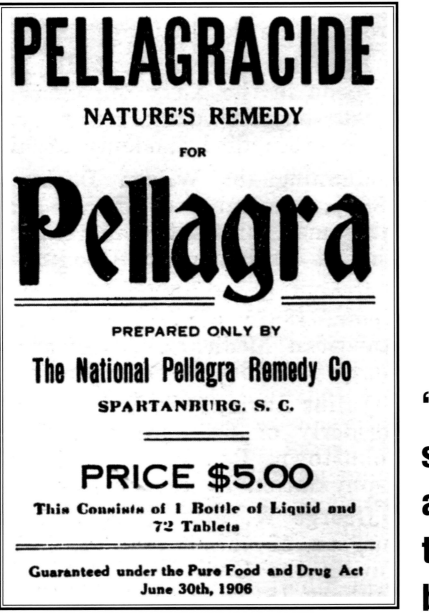

PELLAGRACIDE

NATURE'S REMEDY

FOR

Pellagra

PREPARED ONLY BY

The National Pellagra Remedy Co

SPARTANBURG. S. C.

PRICE $5.00

This Consists of 1 Bottle of Liquid and 72 Tablets

Guaranteed under the Pure Food and Drug Act June 30th, 1906

"My sufferings are greater than I can bear."

Georgia, June 1913

Kittie Tyner, age thirty-five, had been feeling ill. When she visited her doctor, he told her that she had pellagra and that there was no cure.

A few mornings later, when Kittie didn't come out of her room as usual, her relatives went in to check on her. Kittie was gone. She had pinned a note to a dress lying on a chair. In pencil, she had written, "My sufferings are greater than I can bear." She finished the note by saying that her family could find her body in the well next door.

5.

White lines mark the sharp change between normal skin and the rash on the girl's face and hands, a characteristic that makes the pellagra rashes different from sunburns and other skin diseases.

GOLDBERGER ON THE CASE

"You are preeminently fitted
for this work."

—*Surgeon General Rupert Blue*

In **1900, pellagra** was unknown in America. By the end of 1913, it had taken center stage. Newspapers and magazines regularly carried stories about the cursed pellagra victims. Dozens of researchers and doctors wrote articles and books on the subject.

Despite all the attention, no one had proved what caused the disease or explained why thousands of people became sick. The epidemic seemed unstoppable. New cases appeared in places where pellagra had never been seen before. The lucky ones recovered from an attack only to develop it again the next year. Many others died.

The Bureau of the Census records showed 30 percent more pellagra deaths in 1913 than in the year before. The actual death rates were significantly higher because the count included only states and cities that officially registered their deaths. Most of the Southern states, where pellagra hit hardest, were not included in the count.

Mississippi was one Southern state that collected statistics about pellagra. In just six months of 1913, its doctors diagnosed the disease in more than 1,300 people. Another 268 died. In Alabama, 500 people died of pellagra in 1913, putting it fourth behind tuberculosis, pneumonia, and typhoid fever in deaths from infectious disease.

Pellagra's impact on the nation went beyond the deaths and medical care for the sick. People who were weak with pellagra couldn't work. Mississippi estimated that pellagrins missed an average of six to twelve weeks of work each year because of their illness. When they didn't work, they didn't get paid, and that pushed them and their families into poverty.

The state mental institutions couldn't handle all the insane pellagrins. The sick sometimes had to be taken to county jails until space opened up in the asylums—usually when a patient died.

He looked fit and healthy . . . except for the dry, peeling rash.

Arkansas, Fall 1913

J.S.U. was a twenty-two-year-old college student whose father and grandmother had both lost their minds. In fact, his father had recently escaped on the way to the insane hospital and hadn't been seen since.

The young man had no sign of mental illness himself. He looked fit and healthy . . . except for the dry, peeling rash extending from the back of his hands to his elbows. He'd had the same rash every spring since he was sixteen, along with diarrhea and a sore mouth. This year, the symptoms lasted longer than ever before.

In early fall, J.S.U. thought he was better. But in November, he felt so depressed that he tried to kill himself. His family immediately took him to the State Hospital for Nervous Diseases.

The doctors diagnosed pellagra and gave him arsenic-based medicines. J.S.U. slipped into a coma, and three weeks after arriving at the hospital, he died.

The PHS Ramps Up

At the urging of Southern leaders, Surgeon General Rupert Blue expanded the detective work started by Dr. Claude Lavinder. He proposed running a hospital for pellagrins, with an attached laboratory, to discover more about how the disease affected the human body. Congress granted the funds to open the U.S. Pellagra Hospital in Spartanburg, South Carolina, in the same building the Thompson-McFadden Pellagra Commission had used.

The PHS operated this pellagra hospital in Spartanburg, South Carolina. Starting in 1911, special pellagra hospitals opened throughout the South because many regular hospitals refused to admit pellagrins, who some doctors considered contagious and incurable.

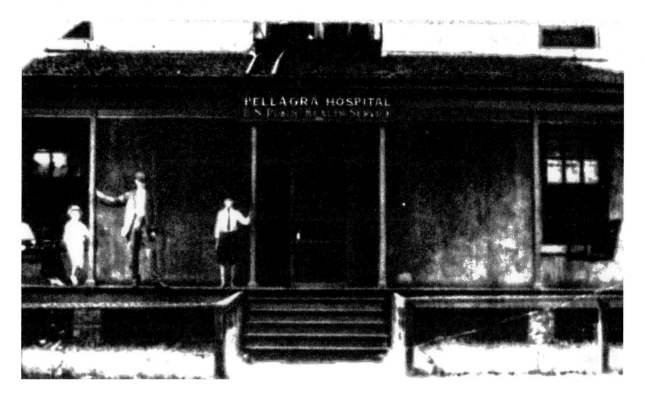

Blue also increased the manpower in the PHS Hygienic Laboratory in Washington to study the biology and chemistry of pellagra. He added researchers in the field to investigate the disease where its victims lived.

The surgeon general needed a leader to head the staff of forty-one pellagra investigators. After more than five years, Claude Lavinder was frustrated by his failure to find pellagra's cause. He requested a transfer to another job within the Public Health Service. Blue turned to thirty-nine-year-old Dr. Joseph Goldberger, one of his best epidemiologists.

Goldberger had been with the PHS for nearly fifteen years and was an expert on infectious diseases. He had earned a reputation for finding clues about how and where epidemics started that other researchers overlooked. Blue felt confident that Goldberger would be the one to find a way to stop pellagra.

In February 1914, the surgeon general sent a letter to Goldberger, putting him in charge of "one of the knottiest and most urgent problems facing the Service."

Immigrant Boy

Joseph Goldberger was born on July 16, 1874, in Europe's Austro-Hungarian Empire. His father, Samuel, herded sheep near Giralt, a small town in what is now Slovakia.

Disaster struck when disease wiped out the flock. Samuel decided that he could make a better life for his wife and six children in the United States, where his two older sons, Jake and Max, had already moved.

In late November 1883, the family arrived in America through New York's Castle Garden Emigrant Landing Depot. Joseph was nine years old and spoke only German.

Like many other Jewish immigrants from Eastern Europe, the Goldbergers settled in the crowded Lower East Side of Manhattan in New York City. Samuel opened a grocery store, and Joseph and his younger brothers helped with deliveries.

In America, the Goldbergers first lived in an apartment in one of these buildings on the Lower East Side of Manhattan.

Joseph Goldberger, about age twenty-two. He was over six feet tall and lanky.

The Goldbergers encouraged education, and young Joseph was a bright student, particularly in math and science. After graduating from school at age sixteen, he entered the College of the City of New York to study engineering.

One day, when Joseph was eighteen, a friend talked him into attending a lecture at New York University's Bellevue Hospital Medical College. The professor's talk about the human body electrified Joseph . . . and changed his life. He realized the path he wanted to follow was medicine, not engineering.

Joseph's parents couldn't afford to send him to medical school. They now had seven children to support. So Joseph borrowed the money from his half brother Jake, who ran a grocery store in New Jersey.

In the fall of 1892, Joseph began his medical studies at Bellevue. He spent extra time in the laboratory and library, eager to learn as much as he could. At the end of the three-year program, Dr. Joseph Goldberger graduated with honors.

In 1897, after an internship at Bellevue Hospital, Goldberger set up a medical practice in his parents' New York City apartment. Unfortunately, things did not go according to his plan, and he attracted almost no patients. A fellow doctor suggested that he move to a smaller city with fewer physicians as competition. Goldberger picked Wilkes-Barre, Pennsylvania, a thriving city about three hours away.

Business was definitely better there, and many people in need of medical care visited him. But it didn't take Goldberger long to see that a private practice wasn't for him. He wanted to do more medical research, performing experiments and doing lab work to figure out better ways to treat patients. He'd had a taste of it at Bellevue, and he liked the challenge.

One of his friends mentioned that the U.S. Marine Hospital Service was looking for medical officers. This work was exactly what Goldberger wanted, so he applied.

Female immigrants pass through a line at Ellis Island in New York.

Epidemic Sleuth

In June 1899, the Service invited Goldberger to enter the next phase of its hiring process. He traveled to New York City, where he spent a week taking difficult written and oral exams. Some of the men failed the tests, but Goldberger passed them and advanced to the second week of testing. At a nearby hospital, he had to diagnose illnesses in patients and identify microorganisms under a microscope.

Goldberger heard that only a small percentage of applicants succeeded in passing all the tests. A month later, he found out that he was one of them. Soon after his twenty-fifth birthday, Joseph Goldberger received a letter informing him that he had been accepted into the Marine Hospital Service as an assistant surgeon.

His first assignment was examining immigrants entering the country at the Barge Office on the tip of Manhattan. A fire had destroyed the U.S. Immigration Station on Ellis Island in 1897.

Medical officers from the Public Health and Marine Hospital Service, looking for contagious diseases or disabilities, examine Jewish newcomers at the immigration station at Ellis Island in 1907. Joseph Goldberger conducted these examinations in 1899.

Along with other Service doctors, Goldberger checked newcomers for contagious diseases such as tuberculosis. He also looked for disabilities, including blindness and heart disease, that might prevent immigrants from supporting themselves.

If he found anyone in poor health, the person would be either sent to quarantine or returned to his or her home country. Goldberger and the other doctors worked quickly in order to inspect the thousands of people arriving each day.

After several months in New York, Goldberger was reassigned to the quarantine station on Reedy Island in Delaware. There, he inspected ships and their cargoes on their way to the port of Philadelphia. Goldberger looked for signs of infectious human diseases and for mosquitoes and rats that might bring contagion into the country. He became a sharp observer, noticing small details as he searched for clues that a ship carried infection.

By the end of two years at Reedy Island, Goldberger wanted new challenges and the chance to tackle epidemic diseases like yellow fever. He requested a transfer from Surgeon General Wyman, and in 1902, he was sent to Mexico to inspect ships heading to American ports.

For the next twelve years, Goldberger moved from one assignment to the next, making a temporary home wherever the Service sent him. He traveled throughout the United States and to Mexico and Puerto Rico, fighting typhus, diphtheria, measles, typhoid fever, yellow fever, dengue fever, and parasites. When he was back at his home base in Washington, he worked at the Hygienic Laboratory. But wherever he was stationed, Goldberger tried to discover how a disease was spreading and how he could stop it.

His job was often exhausting . . . and dangerous. In 1902, while in Mexico, Goldberger became ill with yellow fever. During 1907, in Texas, he caught dengue fever.

In 1905, Joseph Goldberger and these officers of the Public Health and Marine Hospital Service fought the yellow fever epidemic in New Orleans. Goldberger stands in the second row, fourth from the left. Seated third from the right is Rupert Blue, who later became the surgeon general and Goldberger's boss.

While conducting an experiment with monkeys in Mexico in 1909, Goldberger was bitten by a typhus-infected louse. Ten days later, he was burning up with fever, his body covered with spots.

He knew typhus could kill him, but he continued his scientific observations of the disease. Lying ill in bed, Goldberger kept a detailed record of his temperature, pulse rate, rash, and other symptoms. He didn't stop until he became delirious.

After three weeks, the worst was over. Goldberger had survived another deadly disease. "This is childish of course," he wrote in a letter, "but just the same, I have some pride in my 'battle scars.'"

The Mystery of the Itchy Crew Members

In the summer of 1909, Surgeon General Wyman sent Goldberger to Philadelphia to investigate a strange skin disease. For eight summers, a small number of people in the city had developed painfully itchy rashes, similar to hives or chicken pox. Some of the victims were covered with more than ten thousand spots so itchy that they couldn't sleep. Doctors and health officials couldn't figure out what was causing it.

In May 1909, more than a hundred people broke out in the rash, including residents in private homes and crew members on five ships in the Philadelphia harbor. Afraid that the epidemic might spread, the city's health department called the Public Health and Marine Hospital Service.

As soon as Goldberger arrived in Philadelphia on the train from Washington, he went to work. He asked doctors and officials about this outbreak and the previous ones. When did they occur? Who were the victims, and where in the city did they live? How long did the rash last?

Joseph Goldberger poses in his uniform around the time he investigated the mysterious skin disease in Philadelphia.

Next, Goldberger visited the ship-crew patients, who had been taken to a hospital. The men told him that the rashes appeared suddenly yet began to fade within a day after they entered the hospital. Goldberger asked them where they had traveled and what their jobs were on the ships. What had they eaten? Where did they sleep on board?

Goldberger used the clues he gathered and considered the possibilities. Could this be an infection? Not likely. All of the victims on each ship or in each house developed the rash at the same time, so they couldn't have infected each other. Also, the people in the private homes had had no contact with the ship crews.

Could it be food poisoning? No, the victims had eaten the same food as family members or co-workers who didn't get the rash.

Could a chemical poison or plant toxin have brought on the rash? None of the victims had been exposed to those.

Goldberger had one last suspect—an insect or a spider. Bites or stings from mosquitoes, bedbugs, and fleas caused itchy red bumps, too. He decided that the attacking bug must be nearly invisible, though, because no doctor or patient had noticed it.

With an idea of what he was looking for, Goldberger examined the victims' ships and homes, searching for a common factor. In each place, he spotted mattresses stuffed with straw. He learned that only the victims, not others in the ships or houses, slept on these mattresses.

Goldberger had a hunch. Pushing up his sleeve, he stuck his arm between two of the mattresses and held it there for an hour. The next morning, his arm was covered in the same itchy rash he'd seen on the patients.

Something miniscule in the straw must have caused the rash. Goldberger shook some mattress straw over a flour sieve to separate out the dust and finest material, including—

he hoped—the tiny culprit. He taped a petri dish full of the powder under his arm for an hour. By the next day, his skin had broken out in the rash.

Using a lens, Goldberger carefully examined the powder in the petri dish. There they were—several mites, creatures related to ticks and spiders. He showed them to an entomologist, who confirmed that these particular mites infested grain plants. That explained why they were in the straw.

Goldberger wanted to be absolutely sure that he had found the cause of the rash. He put five of the mites on a small piece of curved glass and taped it under the arm of a volunteer. Within a day, the man's skin had five itchy bumps. It was the final proof he wanted.

No one had been able to solve this medical mystery for eight years. Goldberger had figured it out in just a few days.

A Personal Life, Too

Early in his career at the PHS, Goldberger met a co-worker's cousin, a young woman from New Orleans named Mary Farrar. Goldberger liked Mary from the start and enjoyed her company. For several years, they exchanged friendly letters while he traveled for his work. Then in 1905, when he was stationed in New Orleans to fight a yellow fever epidemic, he and Mary began dating.

He was Jewish, and she was Episcopalian. He was an immigrant whose parents ran a grocery store. She came from an old Southern family and was the daughter of a wealthy, well-known lawyer. Despite their differences, they fell in love.

When Joseph and Mary announced their plan to marry, their parents were worried about those differences. Mary's father even conducted a background check on Joseph.

After Mr. Farrar received glowing reports about Goldberger, Mary's parents were satisfied that he would be an

Mary Farrar Goldberger (1881–1959) at age eighteen, around the time she met her future husband. Mary attended Newcomb College in New Orleans, Louisiana.

acceptable husband for their daughter. Joseph's Jewish parents overcame their initial concern about Mary's Protestant faith.

With their families' blessing, the couple married in April 1906 and settled in Washington. The next year, they started their family, eventually having three sons and a daughter.

Assignment: Pellagra

In early 1914, Goldberger was working on a diphtheria outbreak in Detroit, Michigan, when he received Surgeon General Blue's orders assigning him to the pellagra investigation. Goldberger understood what this would mean. His assignments had often taken him away from Mary and their children. Once again, he would have to travel from his home in Washington for long periods, and he wasn't looking forward to it. But his job was to protect the public from diseases. Pellagra had to be stopped.

He sent Mary a letter from Detroit telling her about his new orders: "Of course I wrote to Blue that I'd 'go to it.' I must confess, however, that I've never faced anything with greater reluctance. However, there's no use 'grouching.'"

Goldberger had never seen a case of pellagra, and he knew little about it. He read everything he could find about the disease, including the theories of the Italians and the work by Lavinder and Grimm of the PHS. Then he pored over other scientists' research papers and doctors' reports.

Most people in the medical community accepted the infectious theory proposed by the Thompson-McFadden Commission, which blamed pellagra on a microorganism. But after reading the medical research, Goldberger wasn't so sure. He would let the evidence lead him to pellagra's cause.

Determined to solve the mystery before more people died, he set off on his new assignment.

"Her death is most deplorable . . ."

 **outh Carolina, February 1914**

Maud Johnson was nineteen. She had just finished a course in business and found a job when she developed pellagra. Her father had died of it the previous year. Maud's grief-stricken mother cared for her until the end came at eight o'clock on a February evening. The local newspaper announced Maud's burial, adding, "Her death is most deplorable, for she was a young woman . . . bright and attractive."

6

This two-year-old girl has the butterfly rash across her cheeks, as well as darkened fingers.

"I hope that in due time we may help a little to turn on the light and dissipate the fog."
—Dr. Joseph Goldberger

The Observations

During the spring of 1914, Joseph Goldberger headed to the South. He had to see the disease in order to understand it. He had to meet pellagra's victims face-to-face.

Goldberger traveled by train and occasionally by car to places where he knew he'd find people with pellagra: the mill villages, farming areas, and institutions (insane asylums, hospitals, orphanages, and prisons).

Wherever he went, Goldberger asked doctors and officials about the number of pellagra cases they'd seen, when they occurred, and how many had been fatal. He searched for typical causes of infectious disease—poor sanitation and insects—and found plenty of both. People lived in close quarters that were often dirty.

But in the hospitals for the insane, he noticed an important detail. The nurses and other staff never caught pellagra, although they spent many hours each day and night with pellagrins. They seemed to eat the same food as the sick. In some places, they even slept in the same building.

Goldberger had fought contagious-disease epidemics for years. This wasn't the pattern of an infection spread by person-to-person contact or insects. He wondered: "If pellagra be a communicable disease, why should there be this exemption of the nurses and attendants?"

He decided to look carefully for differences between the staff members and pellagrins. Goldberger visited the Georgia State Sanitarium in Milledgeville, the largest insane asylum in the South, where more than a third of the deaths were due to pellagra.

During mealtime, he stood at the side of the dining room, observing the staff and patients. The food brought from the kitchen was the same for both groups, who sat at different tables. But as he watched, Goldberger saw that the nurses and attendants had first choice of the food. They helped themselves to all the lean meat, eggs, and milk. These items cost the sanitarium more, so it didn't serve enough for everyone. The only food left for the patients was biscuits, cornmeal, and grits. This happened day after day. The patients lived on a monotonous diet without animal-protein foods.

Next, Goldberger traveled to an orphanage in Jackson, Mississippi, where a third of the 211 orphans had pellagra. He was surprised to find that almost all the sick were between the ages of six and twelve. None of the staff and only 3 of the 91 children of other ages had the disease. What would explain this? Goldberger took a closer look.

He inspected the rooms where the orphans slept and spent their days. He found that all of them lived under the same overcrowded conditions.

Goldberger made notes about what the children ate at each meal. All were served some vegetables, though rarely any fresh fruit. But apart from those foods, he discovered that the orphans' diets were very different.

The matrons gave children younger than six a cup of milk three times a day. The menu for teens was designed to keep them strong enough to work, and it included more meat. The children in the middle received biscuits, cornmeal, corn grits, and syrup, but less meat and milk than the others.

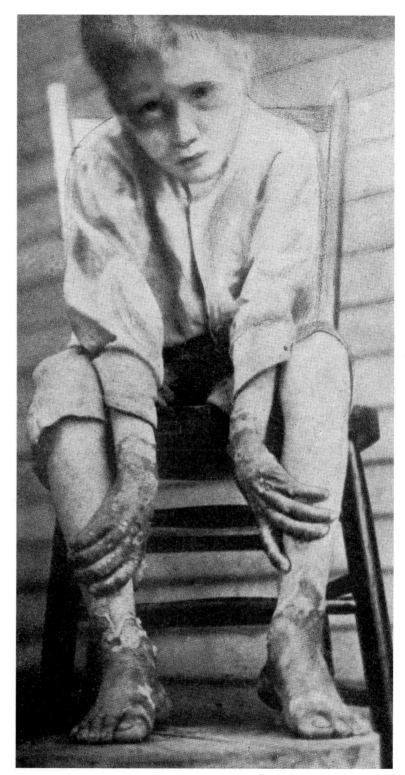

This boy lived in an orphanage where he developed pellagra.

Once again, Goldberger was struck by a single difference between people who got pellagra and those who didn't: the amount of animal protein they ate.

He felt confident that he was on the right track to finding pellagra's cause. When he returned to his home in Washington for a visit, his wife, Mary, saw that "the light of battle was in his eyes."

Georgia, March 1914

S.R. had always been reasonably healthy, but for the past year something seemed wrong with her body. She didn't have the energy to do her housework, her tongue was sore, and her hands were red. After a while, she developed a never-ending headache. Constant diarrhea caused her to lose weight.

Her doctor told her that she had pellagra, and he sent her to the hospital. But that didn't seem to help S.R. Her diarrhea became more severe, and she was emaciated. After nearly a month in the hospital, the woman couldn't think clearly or remember what had happened the day before. She lay in bed with her eyes nearly closed and her arm or leg occasionally twitching.

Less than two days after her mental deterioration began, S.R. died.

Kentucky, April 1914

When one of Mrs. Chilt Sandusky's two small children became ill, the mother called the doctor. During his house call, he spotted redness on Mrs. Sandusky's arms. Recognizing pellagra, he broke the news to the unsuspecting woman. "She was shocked almost into unconsciousness," reported the Lexington newspaper.

For a year, doctors treated Mrs. Sandusky. But despite a short period of improvement, her pellagra symptoms worsened, first affecting her mind and then killing her.

The Hypothesis

Goldberger traveled through the South for several weeks. He saw poor families on farms and in mill villages eating the same diet as the orphans and asylum patients—*meal* (cornmeal baked into bread), *meat* (fatback, from the fatty layer on a pig's back), and *molasses* (syrup).

The families ate the 3-M diet for three meals a day all year. They occasionally added vegetables like collards and turnips, if they could get them. To these Southerners, the 3-M foods tasted delicious, were easy to prepare, and filled a hungry stomach. They were also cheap enough for a poor family to buy.

From what he had seen and read, Goldberger knew that the wealthy and the urban poor didn't live solely on these 3-M foods and rarely got pellagra. In his mind, he began putting together his observations of pellagra victims with the scientific reports he had studied. Goldberger was aware of Polish chemist Casimir Funk's 1912 writings on deficiency diseases. He had read the comments by PHS's Grimm about Southern pellagrins' diets. He remembered that even the Illinois Pellagra Commission, which supported the infectious theory, had noted an increase in pellagra in an asylum after it cut back on meat servings.

The key to pellagra's cause was clear to Goldberger: a diet high in corn or other cereals and low in animal-protein foods. But his idea was still only a hypothesis, and he would have to prove it.

In June 1914, just a few months after he began his investigation, Goldberger presented his hypothesis in a report published by the PHS. Pellagra did not spread from person-to-person, he wrote. It was not caused by infection from a microbe or an insect or by corn

Some doctors referred to the butterfly-shaped rash on the girl's neck as the Collar of Casál, named after the first doctor to write about pellagra.

and corn products. Instead, he proposed, pellagra was due to eating the unbalanced 3-M diet.

Until the cause was definitely proved, Goldberger suggested trying "to prevent the disease by improving the dietary of those among whom it seems most prevalent." He recommended more fresh meat, eggs, and milk and less cereals and canned foods.

Georgia, August 1914

When the woman was brought to the state sanitarium, she was psychotic. Doctors recognized the signs of pellagra—diarrhea, sore mouth, and rash—and put her in the infirmary.

Following the recommendations in Goldberger's report, they fed the woman half a dozen eggs and a half-gallon of milk each day. They also gave her steak, chicken, vegetables, and crackers. Within a few weeks, she had improved remarkably. Her pellagra symptoms disappeared, and she gained weight.

South Carolina, September 1914

J. A. McNeeley had a job at the Pendleton Cotton Mill and lived in the mill village. His entire family, including the five children, was stricken with pellagra. When Mr. McNeeley became too sick to work, the family had no means of support. He was forced to ask the county commissioners to accept all seven of them into the hospital at the county home (a government-run care facility). The commissioners agreed to take in the family as charity cases.

The Orphanage Test

Goldberger couldn't afford to waste time. Southerners were sick and dying. That summer, he designed an experiment to test whether feeding people a nutritious diet could really prevent pellagra.

In September, he started with orphans. At each of two orphanages in Jackson, Mississippi, dozens of children developed pellagra every spring and summer. Their symptoms disappeared in fall and winter, but at least half of the sick became ill again the next spring.

Goldberger was appalled at the orphanages' fall and winter menu. For breakfast, the children were given grits, biscuits, gravy, and syrup. For lunch, they had one roll. At dinner, they got boiled turnips, cabbage, sweet potatoes, and corn bread. "The poor, helpless children . . . ," he observed sadly, "are not as well fed as are the cattle."

Using PHS funds, Goldberger supplied more beans and peas as well as enough animal protein to both orphanages so that all children ate an egg daily and meat three or four times a week. The children under age twelve drank milk at least twice a day. Goldberger reduced the servings of corn products like grits and corn bread.

He made no changes to hygiene or sanitation or any other living condition.

As part of his research, Goldberger changed the menu at two orphanages in Jackson, Mississippi. This photograph shows children at a similar orphanage in Iowa in 1918.

A couple of weeks after the diet test began, Goldberger and his PHS assistant were walking through one of the orphanages when a boy ran up to him. "Are you all giving us all the things to eat?" asked the boy, who looked about seven or eight years old to Goldberger.

He replied that they were and asked if the boy liked the food.

"Oh! indeed we do," exclaimed the boy. "I hope you won't stop!"

Goldberger didn't stop. He continued supplying the extra food throughout the winter and spring. In June 1915, he returned to the orphanages to check on the experiment.

"They are all well!!!" he wrote Mary from his hotel near the Mississippi orphanages. None of the children at the first orphanage developed pellagra or suffered a relapse. At the second orphanage, only one child became sick, and he had had pellagra before. The results were stunning.

"We surely can stop pellagra by a correction in diet," Goldberger told Mary. "The work . . . will be a mile-stone in the history of preventive medicine. The knowledge we have gained is sure to save thousands of lives annually . . . not to mention the misery of many years of suffering and ill health of thousands of others."

Arkansas, June 1915

The governor's office reported that two children died of pellagra at the Baptist orphanage in Monticello, Arkansas. Twenty-five other orphans between ages two and eighteen were ill with the disease.

The Sanitarium Experiment

At the same time they were conducting the orphanage test in Jackson, Goldberger and his PHS assistants ran a separate test at the Georgia State Sanitarium. They chose a

> **"We surely can stop pellagra by a correction in diet."**

group of 72 female patients, both black and white. The women were all pellagrins, and a quarter of them had suffered at least two attacks.

Starting in the fall of 1914, Goldberger fed the women more animal-protein foods (milk and fresh beef) than they had been getting before. The patients also received more peas and beans and less corn and syrup. A control group of other female patients continued to eat the mental asylum's regular menu.

At the end of April 1915—during the spring pellagra season—Goldberger got his first hints that the diet test might work. None of the women on the special diet had yet shown a return of their pellagra symptoms. He felt confident enough to predict: "My inferences as to the effects of diet will be proven to be 100%+ correct."

As the summer went on, Goldberger became more excited by the results he was seeing at the orphanages and sanitarium.

This 1914 insane asylum ward is similar to those at the Georgia State Sanitarium, where black and white patients were placed in separate wards. Elsewhere in the South, blacks and whites were treated in different institutions.

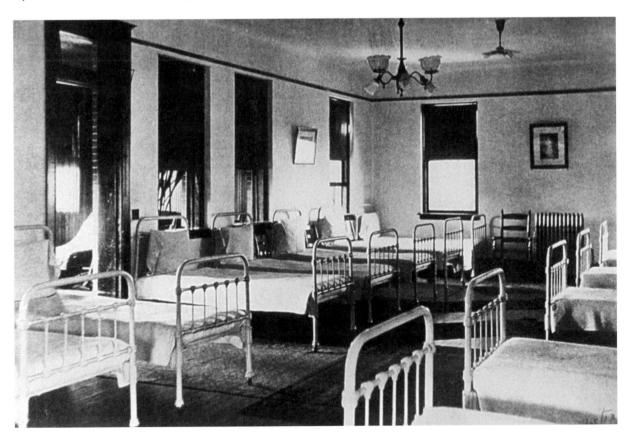

Because mental disorders are a symptom of advanced pellagra, some patients in insane asylums already had the disease when they were admitted. Others developed it after they entered the asylum because of the inadequate diet they received.

He and his team had stopped pellagra attacks by simply feeding people nutritious food. "It almost seems as if it were possible by this means to bring the dead to life," he told his wife.

By October, Goldberger learned that his prediction about the sanitarium's patients was right. All remained pellagra-free. He had cured them! In the control group receiving the regular institutional food, half of the women were sick with the disease.

"The results clearly confirm all my deductions," Goldberger wrote. "He who still doubts that pellagra is 'essentially of dietary origin' is hopeless."

Georgia, May 1915

Mrs. J. W. Pope's pellagra was killing her. Doctors told the woman's husband that there was nothing they could do. Mr. Pope tried to care for her, but he was exhausted from too little sleep. To make matters worse, he was forced to quit his job because he had no one to leave her with.

The Associated Charities gave the family some groceries, but it wasn't enough. "I have been begging eggs and sweet milk from the neighbors to feed her on until I am ashamed of myself," Mr. Pope told the local newspaper. "My wife is dying, my five children are hungry and my house rent is about due."

The Pellagra Squad

Goldberger believed that his diet tests had convincingly shown how to prevent and cure pellagra. But many American doctors still supported the infectious disease theory. They argued that people caught pellagra after a poor diet had weakened their resistance to its infection. Because of this view, pellagrins in some places were being quarantined, and the public was afraid of catching the disease.

Goldberger wanted to put an end to the faulty thinking as quickly as possible. He planned an experiment in which he would *cause* pellagra by feeding people the 3-M diet.

He had one problem, though. According to some reports, as many as half of all pellagrins died from the disease. If his hypothesis was right, Goldberger would bring on pellagra in a healthy person. Where could he find human volunteers willing to take the risk of death?

Help came from Mississippi's Board of Health and Governor Earl Brewer, who was worried about the state's exploding pellagra rate. In 1914, Mississippi had 11,000 pellagra cases, and more than 1 in 10 pellagrins died. More Mississippians suffered from pellagra than from tuberculosis and pneumonia, two major killer diseases.

Governor Brewer found the volunteers at the state's Rankin Prison Farm for white convicts. He offered pardons to prisoners if they were chosen and participated in Goldberger's experiment.

These convicts were perfect for the experiment because none of them had ever had pellagra. They worked the farm and produced a steady supply of fresh and nutritious food for the prison, including meat, milk, and green vegetables.

In early 1915, Goldberger chose twelve healthy men from the volunteers. Seven of them were serving life terms for murder or assault. He told the prisoners the purpose of the experiment and explained that they would be eating a diet that might make them sick. After six months of eating these foods, he promised, they would be pardoned and freed.

Goldberger planned the experiment so that he tested diet changes, and nothing else. He had to protect the men from exposure to infections or disease-carrying insects.

In February 1915, he separated the volunteers, called the Pellagra Squad, from the rest of the prisoners. They lived in their own cottage kept thoroughly clean and equipped with window screens. The men were required to wash their hands and face before eating, to bathe, and to wear fresh clothing. To make sure that these conditions were maintained, Goldberger's thirty-year-old assistant Dr. George Wheeler lived at the prison with his new wife, Agnes.

The Prisoners' New Diet

Wheeler monitored the Pellagra Squad for several weeks, checking that nobody showed any pellagra symptoms. Any man with the disease would have been taken out of the experiment. During this period, the volunteers continued to eat regular prison food, which provided adequate nutrition and included meat, fresh vegetables, and milk.

Goldberger planned to run the feeding experiment from April to October 1915, which was the time of the year when most pellagra cases appeared. In mid-April, the volunteers had their last regular prison meal. Then they began eating the monotonous 3-M diet of corn bread, corn grits, pork fat, and syrup. In addition, they were served biscuits, rice, and small amounts of vegetables such as sweet potatoes and collards. The men were not given milk, meat, or fruit. Guards kept an eye on them to make sure they didn't sneak other foods.

Goldberger needed a control group for comparison. This way, he would know whether changes in the volunteers' health were due to their new diet instead of infection or something else. The controls were the approximately one hundred other people who lived at the prison farm—prisoners and about a dozen nonprisoners, including officials and their families.

The prisoner controls continued to eat the normal prison food. The officials and their families ate similar food but supplemented it with more milk, eggs, and lean meat.

Goldberger and Wheeler watched the controls for cases of pellagra. Goldberger was especially interested in the health of the women and children in the officials' families, two groups that seemed more susceptible to the disease.

George Wheeler (1885–1981) was born and raised in western North Carolina. He joined the PHS in 1914.

91

Waiting for the Rash

George Wheeler regularly checked the health of the Pellagra Squad. Within a few weeks of starting the experimental diet, all the men had lost weight. They complained of headaches, abdominal pain, and weakness. Goldberger and Wheeler knew that these symptoms could be signs of many different illnesses. The pellagra rash was the definitive proof they needed, and none of the volunteers had it.

In July, halfway through the experiment, one man became sick with an inflamed prostate gland, an illness unrelated to pellagra. He was taken out of the study, which went on with the remaining eleven volunteers.

At the end of August, George Wheeler became discouraged. For months, he and his wife had been living at the prison in a difficult situation. His faith that the experiment would be successful had kept him going. But so far, none of the volunteers showed signs of pellagra.

Governor Brewer had promised the Pellagra Squad that they would be released in October. What if the men didn't develop pellagra by then? The experiment would be a failure.

On September 12, just when Wheeler had nearly given up, he spotted the first rash on a volunteer. Over the next month, six of the men developed pellagra rashes on various parts of their bodies. This was the result Wheeler and Goldberger had hoped to see.

But Goldberger was cautious. He wanted other physicians to confirm the diagnosis, so he invited four doctors familiar with pellagra to examine the prisoners. These doctors agreed that 6 of the 11 men had the telltale pellagra rash. No one in the control group showed any symptoms.

Relieved, Goldberger wrote Mary: "I need hardly tell you that I have been and still am under considerable strain. I do not yet realize that we have really and truly produced pellagra in great big, vigorous men by just feeding them properly or rather 'improperly.'"

On November 1, the prisoners were officially pardoned. Before they left the prison "like a lot of scared rabbits," Goldberger explained to them how to regain their health.

One of the freed men, who had been serving a life sentence, lost fifty pounds during the experiment. "I have been through a thousand hells," he told reporters. "He [Goldberger] said to eat fresh meat, eggs, milk, peas, beans and other vegetables, and you bet I am going to do as he says."

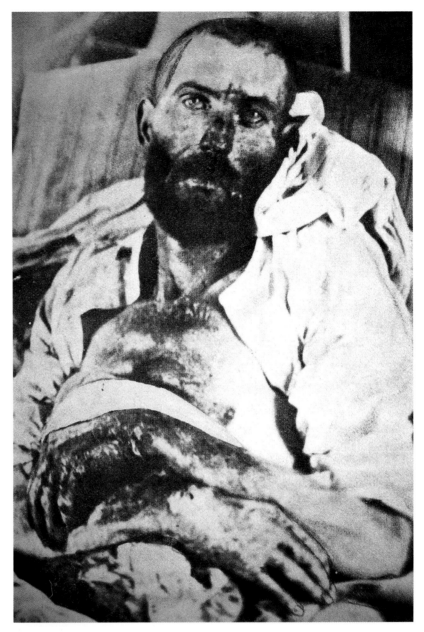

Texas, November 1915

F. G. Myers, age seventy-five, was charged with insanity and put in the county jail's hospital. The jail physician declared that Mr. Myers's insanity was due to the advanced stage of pellagra, and an examining board ordered the sick man sent to a mental asylum. But before Mr. Myers could be moved, he died. He had been in the jail for six weeks. The sheriff's department could locate no relatives.

Goldberger and Wheeler regularly examined the prisoners, looking for a pellagra rash like the one visible on this Tennessee man in 1911.

Mystery Solved

For hundreds of years, pellagra had plagued the world. Yet less than two years after Joseph Goldberger reluctantly took on the pellagra epidemic, he and his PHS team had unlocked the secret of its cause.

Through careful observations and experiments, they found out how to prevent the agonizing disease and how to cure it. The solution turned out to be simple. "Nothing is certain," Goldberger quipped, "except pellagra if you don't feed right."

The discovery that diet could conquer pellagra was met with cheers. Medical leaders around the world praised Goldberger. Newspapers publicized the news with headlines: "Abundance of Protein Food Announced as Remedy" and "Pellagra Cure Found." One magazine columnist wrote: "The Southern states now have the control of this disease in their own hands."

Health officials welcomed the news, too. The boards of health in Mississippi, Louisiana, Florida, Arkansas, and North Carolina planned campaigns to educate their people about how to prevent pellagra by eating a better diet.

Even leading advocates of the infectious theory were convinced. One of the members of the Thompson-McFadden Commission publicly announced at a 1915 pellagra conference that he agreed with Goldberger's findings, congratulating him on his work.

It felt like a victory to Goldberger. After the meeting, he wrote to Mary, "'Diet' wins by a large majority."

The solution to the pellagra mystery came just in time. In July 1914, World War I broke out in Europe. The United States had not joined the fighting, but the South felt the war's effects. Fewer customers were buying Southern cotton, and the prices for the 1914 crop plunged. Many tenant farmers and sharecroppers were hit hard and had little or no money to buy food.

At the end of 1915, the PHS estimated that 75,000 Southerners were sick with pellagra. At least 7,500 of them died that year. In Mississippi, where poor farmers made up most of the cases, nearly 16,000 people had the disease and 1,500 died. South Carolina reported 1,300 deaths.

But now Joseph Goldberger had found a way to end this despair, and he was proud of his accomplishment. "I'm just as pleased and happy over it as I can be," he wrote his wife. "I am sure that the knowledge that we have helped to spread abroad will do an immense amount of good."

He was certain that he had managed "to turn on the light and dissipate the fog" surrounding pellagra. But Goldberger would soon learn how wrong he was.

This nine-year-old carries a heavy sack of cotton as she picks the crop on her family's Oklahoma farm in 1916. During harvest season, the girl picked cotton from 6:00 a.m. to 7:00 p.m. She told the photographer that she didn't like the work.

7

This South Carolina boy had pellagra for three years during the early 1900s. He died ten days after the photograph was taken.

"[They] swallowed in capsules the most nauseating diabolical concoctions."
—*Mary Goldberger*

In 1916, while the war continued in Europe, a battle over pellagra went on in the American medical community. Goldberger had gained the support of influential doctors throughout the country. He had been asked to give a prestigious lecture at the Harvard Medical School and was nominated for the Nobel Prize. In recognition of the pellagra breakthrough, President Woodrow Wilson had invited the Goldbergers to the White House for a Friday evening reception.

Yet the opponents of Goldberger's diet theory remained unimpressed. They continued to believe that pellagra, like most diseases, was caused by germs or poisons. The study of nutrition and its effect on the human body was still new, and many physicians didn't understand or accept it.

Southern doctors led the criticism. They resented how Goldberger connected pellagra to poverty in the South. Physicians from Mississippi and Georgia complained that Goldberger hadn't run his diet experiments long enough to prove anything. Several claimed that he had found a good treatment for pellagra, but certainly not the cure.

An Arkansas doctor wrote that the prison experiment "would have proved more convincing had it been conducted in a pellagra-free territory," not Mississippi. With the high number of pellagra cases in that state, the prisoners were more likely to catch the disease.

A Georgia physician who backed the moldy corn theory denied that a diet low in animal-protein food could cause pellagra. Maybe the prisoners already had pellagra when the study started. Or maybe they never really developed pellagra rashes after all. Another researcher even accused Goldberger of faking the experiment.

What About Wealthy Pellagrins?

Over and over, Goldberger heard the same argument from Southern doctors: they had seen pellagra in wealthy patients who ate nourishing foods, which proved that his faulty diet theory was wrong.

Goldberger had little patience for this opinion. These men, he wrote Mary, "flatter themselves with the belief that they are unbiased 'investigators.' . . . They reason that inasmuch as I can not instantly explain every observation that therefore I must be wrong. It never seems to occur to them that the observation they want explained may be erroneous."

He tried to show them why their thinking was flawed. Well-off pellagra patients are probably picky eaters, he said. They only eat certain foods despite having access to milk, eggs, and meat, and they aren't honest about it when a doctor asks.

Sometimes, Goldberger persuaded a critic. After talking with him, one Tennessee physician checked the diet of his pellagra patients more closely. He later told Goldberger that "former patients who, he had believed, had had plenty of a good diet . . . really didn't eat it."

But Goldberger's efforts weren't enough. He still couldn't convince the many Southern leaders and physicians who were insulted when he accused their region's diet of causing pellagra. A doctor from Mississippi announced at a medical meeting, "Most pellagra patients are negroes, and they have lived better, with rice and beans as their great staple, during the past few years than ever before."

An indignant Tennessee doctor added, "I want to enter my protest against this advertising that the South is starving her people."

This wasn't the kind of advertising that Southern leaders were looking for as they tried to attract industry and business to the region. They didn't want their workers perceived as being weak and sickly as a result of the South's culture and eating habits. It was far better if pellagra was an infectious disease, like typhoid fever, that could be cured and wiped out.

Texas, December 1915

On the day before Christmas, a black woman's body was found in the train depot in Abilene, Texas. Because no one had seen her die, the local justice ordered an inquest. The investigation revealed that the woman was Mary Rice and that she had been traveling from Colorado to Ballinger, Texas. The justice declared that Mary had died of pellagra.

Fighting Back

When his ideas and research were attacked, Goldberger stayed calm. But inside, he felt contempt for his critics. In his view, they were "blind, selfish, jealous, prejudiced asses."

He had expected his experiments' results to prove to physicians that pellagra was caused by diet. Now he realized he would have to do more to get his message "to the plain everyday worker and his wife . . . who are living on 'bread' [corn bread] and molasses and have pellagra."

At every opportunity, he shared this information with newspaper reporters so that ordinary people could read about it. He urged the public to eat less starchy cereal and sweet foods and more lean meat and milk.

Goldberger insisted that pellagra could be completely cured through diet, not fake tonics. "We've been giving our starving people medicine," he announced, "when all they need is food!" Pellagra patients recovered in the hospital, he explained, *not* because of the arsenic-based remedies, transfusions, or other elaborate treatments, but because the hospital was feeding them nourishing, well-balanced meals.

Pellagrins didn't have to move to a cooler climate in order to get well. Those who improved after moving to the mountains or to the North did so because their diet changed and they began to eat more meat, milk, and eggs.

He told the public that they had no reason to fear pellagra. "I can not emphasize too strongly," he said, "the fact that pellagra is not communicable."

This Oklahoma sharecropper and his family pick cotton in 1916. The older two children—ages six and five—together picked twenty-five pounds of cotton a day. Goldberger tried to communicate his message about diet to farmers and mill workers, two groups that suffered from pellagra.

A Pellagra Pill

But Goldberger could see that his statements alone wouldn't silence his critics or reassure worried people. He decided to perform a bold experiment that put to rest the infectious theory once and for all.

He would try to infect himself with pellagra by using skin scales, feces, urine, blood, saliva, and other body fluids taken from pellagrins. These were the materials known to transmit disease in humans. If a pellagra microbe or parasite existed, it would be in one of those substances. In that case, Goldberger would develop pellagra symptoms. If he stayed healthy, he proved that the disease was not contagious.

In April 1916, Goldberger was ready to start his experiment. George Wheeler volunteered to join the test. Wheeler, who had been Goldberger's assistant since 1914, believed in his boss's diet theory and wanted to help prove it.

The two men felt confident that they wouldn't catch pellagra, because they were sure it wasn't contagious. Besides, this kind of experiment had been done before.

In 1808, an Italian physician tried to infect himself with saliva, blood, and dried skin from pellagrins, but he didn't get pellagra. In 1909, a doctor at an Alabama hospital for the insane performed the same experiment without any reaction. In 1910, Goldberger himself tried it on rhesus monkeys while he was working at the Hygienic Laboratory in Washington. He and a colleague injected the monkeys with blood and spinal fluid from pellagrins, and none of the monkeys became sick.

Still, until they tried to infect themselves, Goldberger and Wheeler couldn't be certain what would happen.

They started their contagion experiment at the U.S. Pellagra Hospital in Spartanburg, South Carolina. For a source of body materials, Goldberger picked out a female pellagrin who had come to the hospital eleven days earlier. She was weak and had diarrhea and skin sores.

Taking turns, he and Wheeler swabbed the inside of her nose with a cotton stick. They immediately rubbed the mucous over the inside of each other's nose. Next, they drew blood from a vein in the woman's arm and injected each other in the shoulder with her blood.

For the next two days, the shoulder muscles in both men were sore and stiff. But neither felt any other effect.

Three days later, Goldberger traveled to an insane hospital in Columbia, South Carolina. He obtained feces from a man with a severe case of pellagra. Two female pellagrins—one suffering a serious attack and the other a mild one—supplied skin scales and urine.

Goldberger made a doughy pill by combining wheat flour and a concoction of the fresh feces, urine, and skin scales. Then he swallowed it on an empty stomach. He ate some baking soda to counteract the stomach acid that would kill microbes, if any were there.

Three days after taking his pellagra pill, Goldberger developed diarrhea. It lasted about a week. Then he was ready for the third part of his experiment.

The Parties

Fourteen of Goldberger's friends and PHS colleagues had asked to join the contagion test. Like Wheeler, they realized its importance to the health of the country. Most were doctors, including Goldberger's assistant for the diet experiment at the Georgia State Sanitarium and the head of the Hygienic Laboratory in Washington.

Mary Goldberger wanted to be part of it, too. She later said, "I begged to be one of the volunteers. . . . This was an act of faith; it took no courage." She was the only woman who participated in the experiment.

For the third test, Goldberger invited Mary and four of the volunteers to a "filth party"—as he called it—at the

They drew blood from a vein in the woman's arm.

pellagra hospital in Spartanburg. On a May day, Goldberger ate a pellagra pill and rubbed a pellagrin's mucous in his nose. The other men did the same. When it was Mary's turn, they wouldn't let her swallow the disgusting pill or swab her nose. But she joined the others in having the blood from three pellagrins injected under the skin of her abdomen.

After the party, one of the men developed a sore lymph gland near the site of the blood injection. Neither Mary nor any of the others felt side effects.

During the next two months, Goldberger hosted four more filth parties in Washington, New Orleans, and Spartanburg. For each party, a different set of volunteers joined him. He used body materials from a total of seventeen pellagrins, including three children. Three of the patients—a woman, a man, and a nine-year-old girl—died within a few weeks of providing urine and feces.

The volunteers did not avoid contact with pellagrins. In fact, Goldberger, Wheeler, and some of the other doctors were frequently around them. If pellagra were contagious, these men were exposed in two ways.

After seven of these revolting tests, Goldberger

As the father of four, Goldberger was particularly saddened by the death of children from pellagra. This girl later died from the disease.

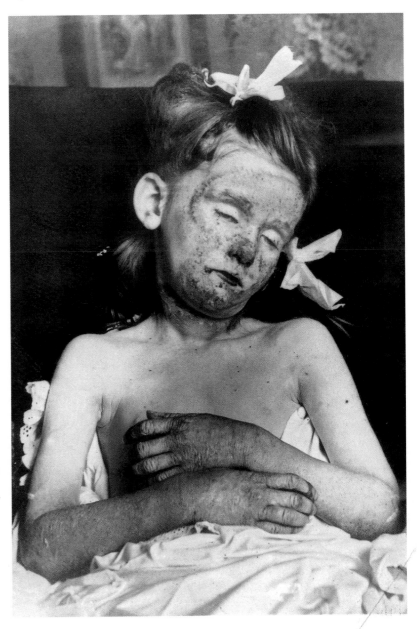

103

was glad when the experiment was over. On June 25, 1916, he wrote Mary from Spartanburg: "We had our final 'filth-party' . . . this noon. If anyone ever got pellagra that way, we three should certainly have it good and hard! We just feasted on the filth. It's the last time. Never again!"

Goldberger and his fellow partiers continued watching for signs of pellagra. Each checked himself daily for redness on hands, neck, feet, face . . . anywhere. But none of them found even a hint of rash. The only side effects anyone noticed were indigestion, mild nausea, and diarrhea for several days after swallowing the pellagra pill.

"When one considers the relatively enormous quantities of filth taken," wrote Goldberger, "the reactions experienced were surprisingly slight."

At the end of six months, none of the volunteers had developed any telltale symptoms of pellagra. To Goldberger, this was solid proof that the disease was not contagious. Surely, his opponents would now believe that faulty diet was the cause.

But some critics still weren't satisfied. One doctor who supported the infectious theory grumbled that Goldberger tested white men in their late twenties to early forties, the least likely group to develop pellagra. If the study had been done right, he said, Goldberger would have used the most susceptible—children and women.

Others charged that the volunteers knew what they were ingesting. Since all of them backed the diet theory, they didn't expect to get pellagra. As a result, their reports of illness or lack of reaction could have been swayed, perhaps unconsciously.

Alabama, May 1916

Pellagra had sickened Mrs. M. B. Harden of Phenix City for an entire year. During the second spring of her illness, her symptoms became intolerable. The fifty-seven-year-old, a wife and mother of three adult children, suffered greatly until her disease killed her at her home on North Railroad Street.

The Cotton Mill Villages

Joseph Goldberger was upset that so many people in the medical community still clung to the conclusions of the Thompson-McFadden Commission. How could the PHS stop pellagra's spread when doctors believed the disease was caused by an intestinal infection, not by an inadequate diet? By refusing to change their views, they were hurting—even killing—their patients.

Goldberger decided to strengthen his argument by performing a new study. Instead of observing pellagrins in institutions, he would focus on people who lived and worked in a community. He picked seven cotton mill villages around Spartanburg, South Carolina.

Goldberger chose this area because of the many pellagra cases in the villages. Spartanburg was also the site of the U.S. Pellagra Hospital where the PHS was already set up and treating patients. The Thompson-McFadden Commission had surveyed these villages a couple of years before. By using the same population of people, Goldberger would be able to directly compare his results and conclusions with the Commission's.

Between 500 and 800 people lived in each of the seven villages. Most were white mill workers and their families.

Housing conditions like this were typical of mill villages during the period of Goldberger's study in Spartanburg, South Carolina. This village is in Concord, North Carolina.

In every village, the residents worked in the same mill, shopped in the same company store, and lived in the same company houses. Yet some households had pellagra, and others didn't. Goldberger wanted to find out the reason for the difference.

When he walked through the villages and saw the houses, he was appalled. He wrote to Mary from Spartanburg: "The pitiful poverty of many of these people it is hard to describe."

The Pellagra Hunt

In spring 1916, Goldberger and his PHS team got to work collecting facts about the villages' residents. Goldberger turned to Edgar Sydenstricker, a thirty-four-year-old statistician and economist who had joined the PHS the year before. Sydenstricker helped determine what information they needed about the people in the villages and the best way to get it.

Sydenstricker organized a group to interview the people in each mill house. The interviewers asked: Did they work in the mill, work in the home, or go to school? How much did they earn and spend? What diseases did they have? What did they eat? How much did their food cost?

Edgar Sydenstricker (1881–1936) joined the PHS in 1915 and became head of the statistical staff, a group that was critical to the Service's investigations. Before coming to the PHS, he had worked as a journalist and studied economics.

This father and the two boys on the right worked in a Virginia mill. In Southern mill villages, it was common for several members of a family to have mill jobs.

The Thompson-McFadden Commission had relied only on the residents' responses about their diet. Sydenstricker got records from the mill owners to verify the foods that residents said they bought in the company store. He and Goldberger suspected that people forgot or were embarrassed to admit what they really ate.

Meanwhile, George Wheeler went on the search for pellagra cases in the seven villages. He tirelessly knocked on the door of every house where a white mill worker lived—about 800 houses in all. Wheeler had grown up in North Carolina, and he used his Southern friendliness to put the residents at ease. He asked to meet all of the family members or boarders in the house so that he could check them for pellagra.

Wheeler counted only those with the distinctive pellagra rash on both sides of the body. He was aware that he was probably undercounting, because pellagrins sometimes didn't get a rash until after they had digestive problems, fatigue, or nervousness. But he and Goldberger didn't want to include a different ailment with similar symptoms. By the time Wheeler finished, he found that about 1 in 10 households contained someone with pellagra.

Who Gets It?

Sydenstricker analyzed the information collected from nearly 4,400 people in the seven villages. When he compared households—those with pellagra and those without it—he found no difference in the amount of corn products people ate. This discovery put to rest the corn theory.

But he did find other key differences in the diets. In the pellagra households, each person ate significantly *less* fresh meat, vegetables, fruit, eggs, and particularly milk and dairy products.

Of all the pellagra cases in the mill villages, two-thirds were children between ages two and fifteen. Their mild symptoms often went unnoticed by their parents and doctors.

After children, the most cases occurred among women ages twenty to fifty-four—eight times more cases than men. Housewives were hit hardest, having four times more pellagra cases than women who worked in the mills.

A woman and her three children sit in the doorway of their dilapidated house in one of the South Carolina mill villages studied by Goldberger and the PHS team.

North Carolina, June 1916

Mrs. R. A. Browning had been sick with pellagra for many weeks. Her toddler daughter, Pearl, only seventeen months old, developed the awful symptoms, too. At the end of spring, tiny Pearl lost her battle with the disease and died.

Was It the Dirty Outhouses?

The Thompson-McFadden Commission blamed the villages' pellagra cases on intestinal infection that spread because of bad sanitation. When outhouses were not built well or cleaned out regularly, feces were exposed to flies and water runoff. To investigate the Commission's claim, Goldberger added a sanitary engineer named Ralph Tarbett to the PHS team.

Tarbett examined the seven villages' water supplies, sewage systems, outhouses, and overall cleanliness. He also counted the number of typhoid fever cases, since typhoid spreads when food and water are contaminated by human waste.

Tarbett's investigation showed no connection between pellagra cases and the quality of sanitation in a village. The Thompson-McFadden Commission's conclusion was wrong. Dirty outhouses did not spread pellagra.

The Pellagra-Free Village

When Goldberger first toured the South in spring 1914, he saw with his own eyes that pellagra was a disease of poverty. Now the PHS study revealed the same thing in the mill villages. Edgar Sydenstricker's analysis showed that, although most mill workers had low incomes, the poorest households had the most pellagra.

Sydenstricker found a puzzling exception, however. One village did not have a single pellagra case, even though it contained many families who were among the poorest of the mill workers. Why was this village spared? The PHS researchers looked closer.

They compared the pellagra-free village with the one having the highest pellagra rate of all seven villages. There was only one difference: the kinds of food the villagers could buy.

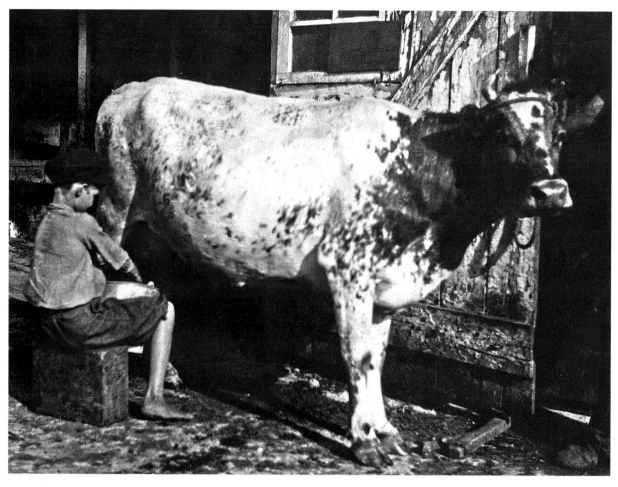

In both villages, people bought food at the mill company store, which rarely sold fresh vegetables, milk, or meat. Near the pellagra-free village, local farmers produced these fresh foods and sold them to villagers. But the high-pellagra village was surrounded by cotton fields, and no locally grown fresh food was available to the mill workers.

Goldberger and his team wrote a report about their mill-village study, which the PHS published. Pellagra could be wiped out, they said, if more nutritious foods were available to poor Southerners. They recommended that farmers in the South grow more food crops and raise animals . . . and cultivate less cotton.

"The single-crop [cotton] system as practiced in at least some parts of our southern States . . . ," they wrote, "will be found indirectly responsible for much of the pellagra."

A boy milks his family's cow in 1916. The PHS saw less pellagra in households that grew vegetables and raised cows or chickens. In some villages, yards were too small for farm animals, or mill owners banned them for sanitary reasons. Other families didn't have time to care for gardens and animals because they worked long hours.

North Carolina, Fall 1917

The forty-five-year-old woman lived on a mountain farm that raised cows and hogs. Her family produced plenty of meat and milk, but she never ate the meat and stopped drinking milk because she couldn't stand its taste. She preferred pastries.

One spring, the woman developed a serious case of pellagra. Her doctor tried to cure her by changing her diet, but she refused to follow his instructions.

Finally, he sent her to the U.S. Pellagra Hospital in Spartanburg, South Carolina. The doctors and nurses there persuaded the woman to eat a better diet, including milk, eggs, and fresh meat. Within a few months, she had recovered.

The Epidemic Continues

Goldberger and the PHS team had made important breakthroughs in the fight against pellagra. Yet the number of cases kept rising. Goldberger estimated that, in 1916, 100,000 people in the thirteen Southern states had pellagra. The disease was now one of the leading causes of death in the majority of these states. In Mississippi, it was fourth; in Alabama, third; and in South Carolina, it was second behind tuberculosis.

From dawn to dusk during the growing season, tenant farmers and sharecroppers plowed the land, planted the cotton, took care of it, and picked it. In many families, the boys plowed the fields, as in this 1916 photograph, and the girls hoed weeds and picked the cotton.

Goldberger calculated that about 5 percent of pellagra cases throughout the South resulted in death. That was still an enormous number of people dying from a disease that could be prevented at the dinner table.

At a time when newspapers regularly described suffering in war-torn Europe, Goldberger was distressed that so many Americans had pellagra because they couldn't afford to eat better. He wrote Mary: "There are many many people living mighty hard in this our own country. I doubt if they are any worse off in Belgium. Someday this will be realized and something done to correct it."

He continued to emphasize in newspaper and magazine articles that nourishing food was the way to fight pellagra. "If all people provided themselves and, at all times, ate a well-balanced diet," he wrote, "pellagra would disappear from the face of the earth."

Most Southern states supported the effort. Mississippi, for example, distributed flyers to its citizens with information about foods that prevented pellagra. It urged schools to discuss good eating habits with students. The state's department of agriculture encouraged people to keep cows and chickens. "Own a cow" became a public health slogan across the South.

North Carolina, Late Spring 1917

The family of eight moved every few months, from farm to farm to lumber camp. The parents seldom earned any money, and the family lived in extreme poverty. Most of their food was donated, and it consisted of cornmeal, flour, fatty pork, syrup, and canned goods. The children hadn't drunk milk in years.

In May, a doctor visiting the lumber camp noticed that the sixteen-year-old boy and twelve-year-old girl had pellagra symptoms. From the look of their skin, he thought they had had previous attacks. Unfortunately, he found that the parents were "ignorant, indolent, and shiftless." They couldn't tell him when or how many times their children had been ill.

The Missing Piece of the Puzzle

Goldberger realized that it wasn't enough to prove that animal protein prevented pellagra. Poor people and underfunded institutions like orphanages and asylums couldn't afford these foods.

The best way to end pellagra was to find the missing piece of the puzzle. What was the pellagra-preventing substance in meat and milk that was lacking in the 3-M diet? And what cheap foods had it, too?

For the sake of thousands of pellagra victims, Goldberger hoped he could find the answers quickly.

Many Southerners—like this family in 1920—ate little or no meat, instead sticking to corn grits, corn bread, and molasses. Two of these children are drinking milk, but some families had no access to milk or other nourishing food.

8
...

This woman's dramatic pellagra rash affects her face, neck, and arms.

His partner in the new detective work was thirty-year-old Georgia native William Tanner, a PHS doctor who had joined in the filth parties. They set up their investigation at the Georgia State Sanitarium, where the patients often got pellagra because of the foods they ate.

For one group of female patients, Goldberger and Tanner added one food at a time to the bland institution diet. They had to wait several months to see whether this had any effect on the women's health.

Goldberger and Tanner tested foods that were high in the known vitamins: tomato juice for vitamin C, cod-liver oil for vitamin A, and cowpeas (black-eyed peas) for vitamin B. They also tried the minerals believed to be necessary for good health, including iron and iodine.

None of these stopped pellagra from developing in the women. The mystery substance was not a known vitamin or mineral.

Goldberger and Tanner ran some preliminary tests with amino acids. But these chemicals were expensive, which limited testing. They also knew less about them because biochemists were still exploring how amino acids affected nutrition.

William Tanner (1888–1969) joined the PHS in 1914, after working as a physician at the Georgia State Sanitarium.

Texas, September 1918

Mrs. W. T. Stephens, age thirty-five, lived with her husband and three children in the small community of Princeton, an hour from Dallas. Stricken with pellagra, she endured its devastating symptoms for as long as she could. Finally, the suffering became too much for her, and Mrs. Stephens ended it the only way she knew how. With a drink of carbolic acid, she killed herself.

A Cotton Crisis

While Goldberger and Tanner tested foods, the United States entered World War I in April 1917. The government urged the public to stay healthy by eating better. The National War Garden Commission published posters that read "The Seeds *of* Victory Insure *the* Fruits *of* Peace," encouraging people to grow fresh vegetables. These home gardens also freed up farm-grown food for the soldiers. The states spread the message to their citizens that a good diet prevented pellagra.

During the war years, the American economy improved and wages rose. Across the South, the number of pellagra cases gradually dropped. In the cotton mill villages around Spartanburg, South Carolina, fewer villagers sought help at the U.S. Pellagra Hospital.

For a few weeks during the fall of 1918, the hospital was used instead to treat victims of the influenza pandemic. During 1918–1919, one-third of the world's population was affected and at least 50 million died. In the United States, a quarter of the population caught the flu, which killed about 650,000.

The pellagra work at the hospital started up again by early 1919. But at the end of 1920, the PHS decided to close the hospital for good. When it began six years earlier, the hospital had a waiting list of 500 people who wanted to be admitted to

The Seeds of Victory Insure *the* Fruits of Peace

For Free Book Write to

NATIONAL WAR GARDEN COMMISSION
WASHINGTON, D.C.

Charles Lathrop Pack *Pres.*   Percival S. Ridsdale *Sec'y.*

The National War Garden Commission published posters during World War I encouraging Americans to plant vegetable gardens.

one of the hospital's 45 beds. Now there weren't enough pellagra cases to keep it open.

South Carolina's leading newspaper told readers that the hospital was no longer needed because "Pellagra has practically been stamped out." It seemed as if the pellagra scourge would soon be a memory.

Then in the fall of 1920, the price of cotton plummeted. Farmers had to sell their cotton crop for less than half of what they received the year before. Most couldn't repay their debts, and they had little money left to carry them through the winter and spring. At the same time, the wages for mill workers fell.

Goldberger understood how a weak Southern economy would lead to pellagra outbreaks. He predicted a sharp increase in cases during the following spring.

By early July 1921, he found out that he'd been right. The number of pellagra victims had more than doubled since 1920 and was still rising.

A new surgeon general, Hugh Cumming, had taken over the PHS in 1920. He, too, worried about the fresh pellagra outbreak. Based on Goldberger's warning, Cumming's office released an announcement to the press in late July.

Newspapers around the country reported the alarming story: 100,000 people in the cotton belt, from eastern Texas to the Carolinas, would fall ill with pellagra. At least 10,000 of them would die. Food and medical care must be sent to these people without delay in order "to save the lives of those already ill and to preserve the health of those who will become ill."

People had been reading about pellagra for more than a dozen years. Was the dreaded disease spreading again?

The crisis grabbed the attention of the U.S. president. Warren G. Harding, who had taken office about five months earlier, responded immediately. In a well-publicized statement, he proposed that the PHS and American Red Cross work together to help the suffering Southerners. "It must bring a

shock to the American people," Harding said, "to realize that a great section of their own country . . . is actually menaced with famine and plague."

Propaganda . . . Slander!

The president's words stung Southerners. Many of them still harbored anger about the South's defeat by the North during the Civil War. They had resented it when the federal government, represented by Goldberger and the PHS, insulted their diet and blamed their cotton economy for pellagra. Now Harding, a Yankee from Ohio, had branded the South with poverty and implied that only the North could save it.

Leaders in the South denied that there was a famine or an increase in pellagra. They charged that the PHS misrepresented the situation and misled the president.

President Warren G. Harding (1865–1923) poses on the White House lawn in July 1921, the week before he addressed the pellagra epidemic. Harding, a Republican, was elected president in 1920 and served until his sudden death— probably from heart failure. An autopsy was never performed.

Congressman James Byrnes of South Carolina sent a letter to President Harding that was published in national newspapers. "The average American dislikes to have placed in front of his door a flag indicating the presence of a plague," he wrote, "when as a matter of fact there exists within his home nothing to justify that characterization. And likewise, where there is no famine, he dislikes to be held up as the obje[c]t of charity."

An editorial in a Georgia newspaper proclaimed: "The South is the greatest country on earth. . . . We are seeking no charity."

Still resisting Goldberger's diet theory, some Southern doctors condemned the PHS and President Harding. A Georgia physician alleged that pellagra was unrelated to cotton prices or food shortages. It was due to moldy corn. The editor of the *Southern Medical Journal* labeled the charge of famine and plague as "propaganda" and "slander."

In response to President Harding's proposal, the Red Cross was ready to send in aid to help people in the cotton belt. The Borden Company offered free condensed milk. The Institute of American Meat Packers pledged ten tons of free meat for the PHS to distribute.

Offended by the attack on their region, Southern public officials turned down the help.

By the end of 1921, the number of pellagra cases and deaths in the South soared. In one of the South Carolina mill villages the PHS had studied, more than twice as many people had pellagra that year than in 1920.

Congressman James Byrnes (1879–1972), a South Carolina Democrat, protested President Harding's comments about the South. Byrnes later served as a U.S. senator, associate justice of the U.S. Supreme Court, secretary of state, and governor of South Carolina.

The reaction of Southern doctors and leaders frustrated Goldberger. All his studies and experiments had failed to change the wrongheaded attitudes and actions that led to pellagra outbreaks. He later told a journalist, "I'm only a bum doctor, and what can I do about the economic conditions of the South?"

More than ever, he saw how important it was to find the pellagra-preventing substance, the foolproof way to save people from the disease.

South Carolina, 1921

Baxter Haynes was a successful forty-one-year-old doctor who invested his money in cotton. When the price of cotton plunged in 1920, he was wiped out. Baxter was so shocked by his sudden financial ruin that he lost his appetite and couldn't sleep. For more than two months, he lived on hot chocolate and crackers.

Soon he started to have problems with his body. His hands turned bright red, his tongue felt raw, and "floods of saliva poured" into his mouth. His entire digestive system was irritated, and his weight dropped sixty pounds.

He prepared himself for death.

Baxter didn't want to admit to himself that he had pellagra. But when he felt his mind slipping, he realized he was in the last stages of the horrible disease. He prepared himself for death.

His friends persuaded him to go to the hospital, where doctors treated him with medications. When he didn't improve, Baxter decided that Goldberger's cure made more sense. He would "eat it out, feed it out, or die."

Starting with milk, he forced himself to drink and eat a little more each day. It took several months, but Baxter finally regained his health.

Black Tongue

Goldberger knew that the search for pellagra-fighting foods would go faster if he could test animals as well as people. Unfortunately, animals typically used for medical experiments—monkeys and rats—did not seem to get pellagra.

In recent years, researchers had been using dogs to study nutrition. When Goldberger read about these experiments, he noticed that the dogs sometimes developed a drooling mouth, tongue sores, and diarrhea. He wondered if this might be the dog version of pellagra.

In August 1921, while he was visiting Spartanburg, Goldberger heard about two dogs with these symptoms. A local veterinarian told him that the dogs—male and female Chesapeake Bay retrievers—had black tongue, a usually fatal infectious disease.

After the retrievers had died, Goldberger, George Wheeler, and the local veterinarian examined the insides of the dogs' bodies. They found that the lining of each dog's mouth and digestive system was inflamed. It was another clue that black tongue was the same as pellagra.

A few months later, Goldberger and Wheeler decided to try bringing on black tongue in dogs with a pellagra-producing diet. They set up their experiment in a building at the Hygienic

Laboratory in Washington. A big kitchen was outfitted with pots, stoves, and scales to prepare foods. Another room was filled with cages of dogs.

Goldberger and Wheeler fed six dogs a diet similar to what the prisoners had eaten during the 1915 experiment. The diet was high in corn and cereals and lacking in meat. When the dogs wouldn't eat it, a veterinarian recommended adding brewer's yeast to stimulate their appetite. (Brewer's yeast is used by beer-makers to produce alcohol and is slightly different from baker's yeast.)

Several months went by, and none of the dogs developed black tongue. Disappointed, Goldberger stopped the experiment. But he didn't give up. Instead, he and Wheeler tried again with some changes.

Another Attempt

This time, as Goldberger wrote later, "we desired to work with as potent a pellagra-producing diet as possible." They changed a few foods and cut out the yeast because pellagrins didn't eat it as part of the 3-M diet. (Corn bread is made without yeast.)

Within two months of starting the new diet, the dogs showed signs of black tongue—sore mouth, drooling, and loss of appetite. In three months, they were dead of the disease.

It was the proof Goldberger and Wheeler needed. They had found an animal they could use for food tests.

They started the next set of experiments by feeding healthy dogs a diet that brought on black tongue. As soon as a dog showed symptoms, they added one new food.

If the black tongue disappeared, they knew they had a pellagra-preventative food. If the dog died, they crossed the food off their list. After testing many foods, they discovered that those containing the greatest amount of pellagra-preventative substance were lean beef, pork liver, and salmon.

Goldberger hadn't forgotten about their failure to bring on pellagra with the first diet. He was curious about the brewer's yeast, so he fed some to one of the dogs.

What happened next amazed Goldberger and Wheeler. Within four days, the dog's black-tongue symptoms began to go away. The researchers had never seen a reaction that fast to any food they tested.

Had the yeast been responsible for the miraculous recovery?

They stopped feeding it to the dog. The black-tongue symptoms came back. When they fed yeast to the dog again, the animal recovered.

Goldberger and Wheeler had not considered brewer's yeast as a possible pellagra fighter. But by luck, here it was.

The next step was to try it on female patients at the Georgia State Sanitarium. In May 1923, at Goldberger's direction, William Tanner started the test with dried brewer's yeast. Tanner dissolved the yeast in water or syrup and gave it to pellagrins. In two or three days, they improved.

Throughout the next year, the women in the test received a daily dose of brewer's yeast. All of their symptoms went away, and no one had a relapse.

Goldberger and his assistants had found a cure for pellagra!

But Goldberger was baffled about why yeast worked. He had guessed that an amino acid in protein foods might be the key to preventing pellagra. These results forced him to rethink his idea. Brewer's yeast had little protein, yet it contained a powerful substance that stopped black tongue and pellagra. Goldberger gave the substance a name: factor P-P, for pellagra-preventative.

Yeast was the kind of cure and preventative that Goldberger had hoped for. At last, people had an inexpensive way to fight pellagra. The yeast powder could be mixed with a liquid and swallowed. It stored easily and didn't have to

What happened next amazed Goldberger and Wheeler.

be fresh. Companies began to sell brewer's yeast, advertising it as a pellagra cure.

A worker stirs a pot on the large stove in the PHS laboratory used for pellagra research.

Letter from Florida, March 1925

"Dear Doctor Joseph Goldberger,

I want you to write me where I can get 'Dry Brewer's Yeast!' and also tell me how to use it for I sure have got a very bad case of pellagra[.] [I]t is on my hands and arms, feet, and neck and is coming in my face and I sure do want to get something for it[.] [H]ow long do you think it will take this yeast to cure me. . . . Mrs. E. C. Belisle"

The Mississippi River Floods

Goldberger had a chance to conduct a wide-scale test of the yeast cure when a disaster hit the country.

Heavy rains drenched the Mississippi River Valley beginning in August 1926. The stormy weather went on for the next eight months. By early April 1927, the river had flooded one million acres of land.

Levees up and down the Mississippi River were supposed to hold back floodwaters. But in late spring, they burst open. Water deluged millions more acres in twelve states from Illinois to Louisiana.

The Mississippi River floods the town of New Madrid, Missouri, in April 1927.

As water covered rooftops and destroyed towns and cities, 700,000 people lost their homes and farms. Hundreds died. Farm animals drowned, and crops were ruined. The flood caused $1 billion in damage—a third of what the entire federal government spent in one year. Neither the local nor federal governments were ready for such a shocking amount of ruin.

In July, the first pellagra cases showed up in Red Cross camps. Goldberger headed to the area to see how the PHS could help. He and Edgar Sydenstricker, the PHS statistician, traveled through Arkansas, Mississippi, Louisiana, and Tennessee. Because roads were washed out, they could reach some places only by boat.

Main Street in Greenville, Mississippi, is underwater.

In the aftermath of the Mississippi River flood, displaced people in Greenville, Mississippi, live in tents supplied by the Red Cross. Black and white refugees were housed in separate camps.

The Red Cross distributed food—and six tons of pellagra-fighting brewer's yeast—to people whose homes were flooded by the Mississippi River.

Goldberger and Sydenstricker found a heartbreaking amount of pellagra. They estimated that 45,000 to 50,000 people in those four states alone would have the disease by the end of the year. Could brewer's yeast cure the sick and prevent new cases?

On Goldberger's recommendation, Red Cross workers passed out six tons of brewer's yeast with the food distributed to flood victims. At a cost of only three cents a day per person, they mixed a few teaspoons of yeast into juice or milk. Within six to ten weeks, people with pellagra were cured and the number of new cases dropped.

When they saw how well yeast worked, most of Goldberger's critics were finally convinced by his diet theory. State health departments began handing out brewer's yeast in drugstores and at weekly clinics.

Yeast had saved lives. Yet help from the Red Cross and the government didn't reach everyone. By the end of 1927, 120,000 people in the United States had become victims of pellagra.

Children line up at the Milk Tent to get their ration in Vicksburg, Mississippi.

outh Carolina, 1920s

Young mother Jessie Lee Carter lived on a farm with her family. For five or six months, a rash covered her arms, hands, and face. "It burned," she recalled. "It was scaley like a fish." No one else in her family had it.

Her doctor never explained what caused her pellagra, but he said, "'Don't worry, there's plenty of it broke out here.'" According to him, the soldiers came back with it from overseas after the world war.

The doctor told her that "they found the medicine to cure it." He gave her a brownish liquid in a bottle. Jessie took a dose every day, and it cured her.

A *Journey Ends*

At age fifty-four, Joseph Goldberger had devoted more than a quarter of his life to the fight against pellagra. Despite finding the yeast cure, he recognized that the disease was not yet conquered. Americans continued to get sick because they didn't have enough money to eat well or didn't know that their diet could make them ill.

In 1928, Goldberger told an audience of nutrition experts, "The problem of pellagra is in the main a problem of poverty." He couldn't change the economy, but he could find inexpensive pellagra-preventing foods. Goldberger and his assistants continued the food tests with patients at the Georgia State Sanitarium and with dogs at the Hygienic Laboratory. Slowly, the team singled out more foods, including liver extract, a particularly good source of factor P-P.

The results of these experiments convinced Goldberger "beyond reasonable doubt that pellagra is a vitamin deficiency disease." He reasoned that factor P-P was part of the vitamin B complex. People called it vitamin P-P, or vitamin G after Goldberger.

In early fall of 1928, Goldberger didn't feel well, and he began losing weight. His doctors

"They found the medicine to cure it."

For nearly fifteen years, Joseph Goldberger continued his quest to end the pellagra epidemic.

130

couldn't figure out what was wrong, but Goldberger knew it was serious.

As the weeks went by, he became weaker. Eventually, he no longer had the energy to go to the Hygienic Laboratory each day. Despite this, Goldberger kept in close touch with his assistants, discussing the results from ongoing experiments.

His doctors tried blood transfusions to build up his strength. Goldberger's family and PHS colleagues volunteered to donate their blood, but the transfusions didn't help.

On the morning of January 17, 1929, fifty-four-year-old Joseph Goldberger died in the Naval Hospital in Washington, D.C. After his death, an autopsy revealed that he had suffered from a rare kidney cancer. He was cremated, and his ashes were scattered over the Potomac River.

At the memorial service, Surgeon General Hugh Cumming described Goldberger's work as "one of the outstanding contributions to the science of medicine." Others saluted Goldberger for his "keen, scientific mind and . . . a determination rare even among men engaged in medical research."

He had led the Public Health Service's battle against pellagra for nearly fifteen years. Working with his colleagues, he identified its cause and found its cure, saving thousands of lives.

Goldberger was proud of what he had accomplished. Shortly before his death, he told Mary, "I know what I have done, and it is a satisfaction to my soul which no one on earth can take from me."

9
...

Milk in Red Cross school-lunch programs helped to keep children healthy.

CONQUERED

"An ailment which has baffled medicine for centuries has at last been relegated to the curable diseases."
—*New York Times*

Goldberger's battle against pellagra was not yet won. After his death, his capable assistant George Wheeler continued the search for vitamin P-P. Wheeler teamed up with William Henry Sebrell, a young medical researcher who had started working at the Hygienic Laboratory just months before Goldberger became ill.

Using dogs and humans, the two tested foods to find affordable and appetizing ones that helped to prevent pellagra. The PHS eventually published a food list to guide the public and doctors. In addition to brewer's yeast and liver, the list included lean meats, poultry, and fish. Other good sources of vitamin P-P were peanuts, wheat germ, turnip greens, and collards. Most cereals had no value.

Hospitals began treating pellagrins with yeast and liver extracts, saving many lives. But some patients were so ill that nothing worked. Their mouths were too sore to eat or swallow. Many vomited when they tried to force down foods with high levels of vitamin P-P. Even those who had been cured of pellagra had relapses when they went home to eat the same diets that originally made them sick.

Despite the discoveries by Goldberger and his PHS assistants, pellagra cases had more than doubled between 1924 and 1929, and the death rate reached an all-time high in 1928. The PHS estimated that during the final years of the 1920s, 200,000 people in the United States had pellagra. More than 7,000 of them died each year.

The public had been told several years earlier how to prevent pellagra with diet and how to cure it with yeast. Apparently, that had not been enough to make a difference.

William Henry Sebrell Jr. (1901–1992) holds a dog used in the Hygienic Laboratory's nutrition studies. Sebrell became the director of the National Institutes of Health.

Tennessee, May 1930

The five-year-old boy had mild pellagra symptoms every spring since he was eight months old. When his parents brought him to the hospital in Nashville, his mouth was sore and his body was covered with a rough red rash. The boy was unusually small for his age, weighing less than a toddler. The doctors suspected that his yearly pellagra attacks had stunted his growth. At the hospital, the boy was fed brewer's yeast as well as a diet high in protein. After a few days, his appetite came back and his skin improved. After nine days, the rash on his neck and face was gone, and his hands and feet had begun to clear up. The social service department sent the boy home with brewer's yeast and helped his parents provide their son with a better diet than what they had been feeding him.

This PHS laboratory is similar to the one used by Goldberger and his assistants in the search for vitamin P-P and the best pellagra-preventative foods.

The Depression Hits

Beginning late in 1929, the U.S. economy fell into the Great Depression. Banks failed, businesses collapsed, and millions of Americans lost their jobs. The Depression would plague the nation for more than a decade.

In the South, cotton mills had less work, and the owners cut wages and hours. Some mills closed, leaving the workers out of jobs. Many people couldn't afford fresh meat, milk, or vegetables. In the mill villages, sore mouths became a common complaint.

During 1930 and 1931, the cotton crop was ruined by a combination of drought and an attack by the boll weevil, an insect pest. Tenant farmers and sharecroppers were left deep in debt with little money to feed their families and at risk of developing pellagra.

Community health nurses across the South treated people in the mill villages and in rural areas far from medical care. They informed women about the foods that could protect their families from pellagra.

The Red Cross and state relief groups gave out brewer's yeast to eat and seeds for planting vegetable gardens. Nutrition field workers visited homes and showed people how to grow the vegetables and preserve them for winter storage. They also taught schoolchildren about healthy eating habits that prevented pellagra.

None of this guaranteed that everybody would eat the right foods. Many Southerners still couldn't afford them. Others preferred to eat their favorite diet—fatback, corn bread, and molasses—even when they had enough money to buy more nutritious food.

Some people didn't have the space to grow a vegetable garden, or they didn't want to. One North Carolina doctor observed that tenant farmers had gardens, but they didn't spend the time and effort to tend them.

In the early 1930s, at the Goldsboro State Hospital in North Carolina for the mentally ill, 1 in 5 new patients had

Public health nurses visited families in rural areas and mill villages, providing medical care and nutrition information to people who had no access to doctors.

The Red Cross provided food to families facing starvation because of the 1930–1931 drought. The Kentucky widow and her children (top) and the Mississippi tenant-farm family (bottom) depended on this help to survive.

During the drought, Arkansas schoolchildren eat a lunch provided by the Red Cross that includes beef-and-vegetable stew, bread, and milk.

pellagra. In South Carolina, in 1931, 30,000 to 40,000 people had the disease, and nearly 600 died.

Pellagra wasn't going away.

Secret Uncovered

In 1937, new hope came to the pellagra-stricken South from a man in the northern state of Wisconsin.

Conrad Elvehjem was born there in 1901, the son of Norwegian immigrants. After growing up on a farm, Elvehjem attended the University of Wisconsin, where he studied biochemistry and animal nutrition.

When he became a professor at the university, Elvehjem investigated the chemistry of vitamins. He knew that Goldberger and the PHS team had found liver to be an excellent source of the pellagra-preventative factor, or vitamin P-P. Elvehjem set out to identify exactly what the vitamin was, using dogs as Goldberger had.

Elvehjem and his colleagues fed the dogs a diet that brought on black-tongue disease. Then they gave the animals small amounts of various chemicals found in liver, testing one chemical at a time.

When the researchers tried nicotinic acid on one of the dogs, they saw an incredible change. The dog's mouth sores disappeared in just two days. They tested nicotinic acid and its close relative nicotinamide on other dogs, and both chemicals worked in the same astonishing way.

In September 1937, Elvehjem announced that nicotinic acid had cured black tongue in dogs. He had identified the pellagra-preventing vitamin that Joseph Goldberger had been searching for.

Nicotinic acid wasn't a new chemical. It had been used in photography for years. Despite the similarity of the name to the "nicotine" in tobacco, nicotinic acid is a different chemical and has nothing to do with smoking.

Will It Work on Humans?

Dr. Tom Spies was excited when he heard about Elvehjem's discovery. Could nicotinic acid cure his pellagra patients, too?

Spies had experienced the anguish of pellagra when he was growing up in northeastern Texas. Many of his farmer neighbors lived on the 3-M diet and came down with the disease. His best friend's mother died of it.

By the time Spies graduated from college in 1923, Joseph Goldberger had proved that pellagra was caused by a diet deficiency. Early in his medical career, Spies cured alcoholics of pellagra with the Goldberger diet of meat, milk, and vegetables. Later, he pursued his interest in diet and disease by starting a nutrition clinic in Birmingham, Alabama, where he treated pellagra cases.

Now that Elvehjem had found a cure for black tongue, Spies and two colleagues immediately tested nicotinic acid on human pellagra victims. Spies obtained the chemical from Eastman Kodak, a photography company that used it in film processing. The doctors gave it to eleven hospital patients by dissolving the chemical in hot water. If the patient's mouth was too sore to swallow anything, they injected the nicotinic acid under the skin.

The results were rapid and remarkable. Within a day of receiving the chemical, the patients' mouth sores began healing. By the second day, their mouths were normal. After two or three days, the fiery redness of their skin started to fade. Within six weeks, the patients were cured.

Tom Spies (1902–1960) dedicated his medical career to curing nutritional diseases.

Spies was thrilled. He later wrote to Mary Goldberger: "Its [nicotinic acid's] effect on patients, even the most severely diseased, is nothing short of miraculous."

Before the end of 1937, several other groups of researchers reported similar results with hundreds of patients.

Nicotinic acid proved to be a better cure than a high-protein diet, brewer's yeast, or liver supplements. It could be swallowed as a pill or injected into patients who were too sick to take it by mouth. The chemical was simple and cheap, and it worked immediately.

Even after the nicotinic acid cure was found, pellagra continued to strike people of all ages. In this 1939 photograph, a ninety-one-year-old North Carolina woman has a butterfly rash across her cheeks.

Tennessee, May 1938

The little boy had never been a good eater. In March, his parents first noticed a red area over his nose and cheeks. Gradually, the redness spread to his entire face and neck. Sores appeared on his hands, feet, and legs, and he had blisters on his tongue. Next, he developed foul-smelling diarrhea. By May, the boy wanted to sleep all day rather than play. His worried parents took him to the hospital.

The doctor recognized pellagra. She decided to use the nicotinic acid cure for the first time. Every three hours, she gave the boy a liquid form of the chemical to swallow. In ten days, his diarrhea was gone, his skin rash was fading, and he was energetic again.

Building Up Bread

After the discovery of nicotinic acid, government and medical groups pushed a new idea. Why not add the B-complex vitamins—nicotinic acid, thiamin, and riboflavin—to wheat flour, bread, and cornmeal? These were foods that a majority of people ate daily.

When millers ground grain into flour, they removed the grain's outer coating, which contained most of these vitamins. By adding the vitamins back, the nation's nutrition could be improved. Starting in 1938, some bakers voluntarily enriched their bread with yeast, which is high in B-vitamins.

The next year, war broke out in Europe again. American leaders saw that it was only a matter of time before the United States entered the war. When that moment arrived, the country would need soldiers. In fall 1940, young men were required to register for a military draft.

As doctors examined the recruits, they found that at least a quarter of the men were too malnourished to serve as soldiers. Something had to be done to improve the health of the nation's people.

An Alabama sharecropper and his family pose in front of their home in 1939. Sharecroppers had a difficult time earning enough to feed their families. In fact, many Americans did not eat an adequate diet.

GROW IT YOURSELF

PLAN A FARM GARDEN NOW

Rural Electrification Administration, U. S. Department of Agriculture

In May 1941, the National Nutrition Conference for the Defense recommended that white flour and bread be enriched with iron, thiamin, riboflavin, and nicotinic acid. The baking industry was concerned that customers would be afraid to eat anything related to nicotine (from cigarettes) or acid. Those words certainly didn't sound healthy! Conrad Elvehjem helped to choose a different name for nicotinic acid—*niacin*. Soon more than three-quarters of white bread was enriched.

The United States entered World War II in December 1941. In January 1943, the federal government turned its earlier recommendation into a wartime order. It required all commercial bakeries to enrich their white bread.

The order stayed in place until October 1946, a year after the war ended. After seeing the health benefits, many states passed their own bread- and flour-enrichment laws. In other states, bakeries and millers enriched voluntarily.

During World War II, the federal government used posters to urge people to grow their own vegetables.

Vitamin enrichment was a spectacular success. Everyone ate bread and cereal products, including people who couldn't afford meat and milk or who didn't like vegetables. Americans were finally eating adequate amounts of niacin, even if they didn't realize it.

In 1940, right before widespread enrichment started, about 100,000 people in the United States had pellagra, most of them in the South. At least 2,000 died.

By 1944, only 9,000 people in the thirteen Southern states still had pellagra. The number of deaths had dropped to about 1,000.

Alabama, May 1943

The fifty-eight-year-old woman rarely ate meat, milk, or eggs. She didn't like them. During her first pellagra attack, she had diarrhea, dizziness, and a burning mouth. For a month, she was too sick to eat, and she lost fifteen pounds. The pellagra symptoms returned every spring.

After a few years of attacks, the emaciated woman claimed that she heard her dead husband calling her. Her daughter, alarmed by these disturbing mental symptoms, finally convinced her mother to go to Dr. Tom Spies's Nutrition Clinic in Birmingham, Alabama.

Spies prescribed a daily dose of niacinamide (related to nicotinic acid) for a week. By the second day, the woman's appetite returned and she began to smile again. By the third day, her mind was returning to normal and her diarrhea cleared up. Four months after first coming to the clinic, the woman had gained almost forty pounds and was eating a healthy diet that included meat, milk, and eggs.

The Rest of the Story

Pellagra's mysteries weren't completely revealed when Elvehjem identified vitamin P-P as niacin, or vitamin B_3. The truth turned out to be more complicated.

As biochemists analyzed foods for niacin, they learned that milk had low levels. Yet milk was quite effective at preventing pellagra, as Goldberger showed in 1914. How could this be true if niacin was the pellagra-preventing factor?

Vitamin enrichment was a spectacular success.

During the 1940s, several groups of American researchers tackled the question. They discovered that animals can make niacin from the amino acid tryptophan. Even if a person eats low amounts of niacin, he won't develop pellagra if he gets enough tryptophan.

Milk contains tryptophan, which is why it is good at stopping pellagra. Tryptophan also occurs in high-protein foods, such as beef, poultry, and fish. Goldberger had labeled all of these as pellagra-preventing foods.

Back in 1922, Goldberger and Tanner considered tryptophan as a possible factor P-P. But when Goldberger stumbled on brewer's yeast as a cure for black tongue in dogs, he steered the research away from amino acids toward vitamins. No one knew then about the relationship between tryptophan and niacin.

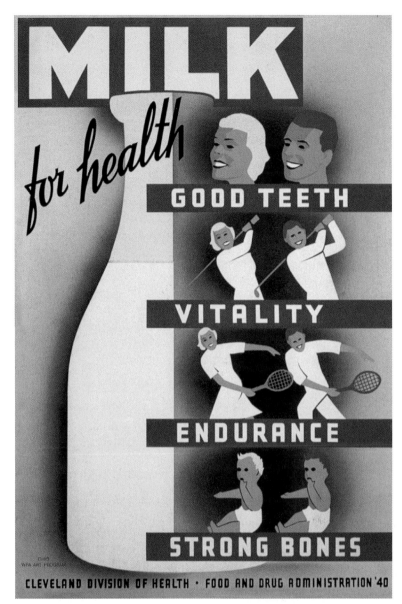

MILK *for health*

GOOD TEETH

VITALITY

ENDURANCE

STRONG BONES

CLEVELAND DIVISION OF HEALTH · FOOD AND DRUG ADMINISTRATION '40

A 1940 poster tells Americans that milk builds strong bones and teeth. A few years later, scientists discovered that milk had another important benefit: it contains the amino acid tryptophan, which prevents pellagra.

The End of Pellagra

Pellagra had been a devastating blight on the South. More than 3,000,000 people became victims during the decades between Dr. George Searcy's warning in 1907 and the beginning of widespread food enrichment in the early 1940s. At least 100,000 Americans died.

The exact number of victims will never be known because most pellagrins didn't seek medical care. During the mill-village study, Goldberger and the PHS team found that in some communities as few as 1 in 6 pellagrins ever visited a doctor for their symptoms.

Enrichment of bread and cereals with niacin finally conquered pellagra. Other changes helped to improve the health of Southerners, too.

After World War II, the South moved away from the cotton-based economy that had helped lead to the pellagra epidemic. The system of tenant farmers and sharecroppers ended. More factories and other industries located in the region, boosting the economy. The mill villages, owned and controlled by one company, soon disappeared.

Farms raised a variety of crops and animals. As the transportation system improved, food from other parts of the country reached the South more quickly and easily. Grocery stores opened up in Southern towns, giving people access to nutritious foods at lower prices.

Areas in the South that had once had thousands of pellagra cases now had just a handful. In 1955, fewer than 100 Americans died of the disease.

Pellagra had baffled doctors for two hundred years, taking scientists down the wrong path time and time again. It proved to be a difficult disease to stamp out. Pellagra kept its stubborn grip on the American South, even though the mystery of its cause was solved. It cursed thousands of victims, even after the secret to its prevention was revealed. It refused to disappear, even when a simple cure was discovered.

Doctors, public health officials, and scientists never gave up the battle. At last, they defeated the disease called "one of the most horrible, pitiful afflictions mankind has ever suffered."

or hundreds of years, doctors realized that certain illnesses seemed to be related to diet. Sailors on long voyages developed scurvy, a disease of bleeding gums, loose teeth, painful joints, and death. Scurvy disappeared when the sailors ate citrus fruit.

In Asia, many thousands of people died from beriberi. They felt weak, lost feeling in their legs, and died from heart failure. By the late nineteenth century, European doctors had connected beriberi to a diet of white rice.

The exact cause of diet-related diseases such as scurvy and beriberi remained a mystery until the first decades of the twentieth century. Then in 1912, Casimir Funk proposed that these diseases were caused by the lack of a vital chemical. He called it a vitamine. *Vita* is Latin for "life." *Amine* is a chemical containing nitrogen. Later, scientists found that not all vitamins contained nitrogen, and the *e* was dropped.

Joseph Goldberger had read about Funk's work before he began investigating pellagra. But in 1914, no one—including Funk and Goldberger—knew that pellagra was a deficiency disease.

During the next three decades, scientists discovered thirteen vitamins that the human body needs in order to work properly. Without them, deficiency diseases develop. By testing humans and animals and by experimenting with chemicals in the laboratory, researchers found the missing factor behind each deficiency disease. Too little vitamin C causes scurvy. The lack of vitamin B_1 (thiamin) leads to beriberi. Low amounts of B_3 (niacin) brings on pellagra.

In the 1930s, researchers figured out how to manufacture vitamins. After that, people could obtain them from a source other than food.

Pellagra Frequently Asked Questions

Do I have to worry about getting pellagra?

Probably not. In the United States, most bread, flour, cornmeal, pasta, breakfast cereals, and rice are enriched. They contain iron and the B vitamins niacin, thiamin, riboflavin, and folic acid. The federal government does not require enrichment, but the majority of states do. Since these products are shipped between states, almost all of them are enriched no matter where you live.

A product cannot be labeled "enriched" unless it contains specific vitamins and minerals set by the federal government. Niacin is labeled on the package.

You can also get niacin by eating animal foods such as lean red meat, poultry, fish, and liver. Plant foods containing niacin include nuts, wheat germ, peas, green leafy vegetables, and tomatoes.

Young people between nine and thirteen need twelve milligrams of niacin a day. After age fourteen, females need fourteen milligrams and males sixteen. Women who are pregnant or breastfeeding, however, need seventeen to eighteen milligrams.

Another way to protect yourself against pellagra is by eating animal proteins high in the amino acid tryptophan. Good sources are meats, poultry, fish, eggs, milk, and other dairy products. Animal proteins contain adequate amounts of the amino acids that the human body must obtain from food.

Plant foods are different. Some are high in particular amino acids and low in others. For example, corn contains very little tryptophan. People who don't eat meat or other animal proteins must be careful to choose foods that together provide enough of all essential amino acids.

Does anyone get pellagra today?

Pellagra is rare in the United States and the rest of the developed world. Most doctors have never seen a case. It can occur in alcoholics, mentally ill patients, and others who eat extremely limited diets. Certain diseases and drugs can interfere with the body's use of niacin or the change of tryptophan to niacin, resulting in pellagra.

During the past twenty years, pellagra outbreaks in underdeveloped countries have usually occurred when a group's regular diet is disrupted by food shortages or war. The disease has appeared in the African countries of Malawi and Angola. Pellagra struck thousands of refugees from Mozambique during the 1990s.

Why is pellagra called the 4-D disease?

The symptoms of pellagra are dermatitis (skin rash), diarrhea, dementia (mental disorder), and death.

How does a diet low in niacin cause these symptoms?

Niacin plays a key role in the chemical reactions that change food into energy. Cells need this energy to function, reproduce, and maintain themselves. The cells in the skin and the lining of the digestive system have the fastest turnover of all tissues in the body. That's where the damage occurs first. Brain cells require high amounts of energy to work properly. When they don't get enough, the pellagrin develops depression, anxiety, confusion, and hallucinations. Finally, if energy levels drop so low that vital organs stop working, the pellagrin dies.

Why did eating a diet of corn bring on pellagra?

Niacin in corn is chemically bound to other molecules. When a person eats corn raw, ground up as meal, or heated, the body can't absorb the niacin. Because corn is also low in tryptophan, the 3-M diet didn't supply enough of either one.

Why don't cultures with diets high in corn have pellagra?

Traditionally, people in places such as Mexico and Central America prepare corn by soaking it in a solution of mineral lime or ashes before cooking. This releases the niacin, making it available to the body once the corn is eaten.

When the Europeans took corn home in the late fifteenth or early sixteenth century, they didn't take back this preparation method. Because people did not cook corn this way in Europe or the American South, their bodies received almost no niacin.

Native Americans who grew the "three sisters"—corn, beans, and squash—ate a varied vegetable diet that provided enough amino acids to stay healthy.

A Mexican woman makes corn tortillas in the late 1800s. Native American cultures used preparation methods that released niacin so that it was available to the body.

Why did the pellagra epidemic spread so fast in the South?

Before 1900, an occasional Southerner probably had pellagra, but most people ate an adequate diet. By the early twentieth century, cotton had taken over the Southern fields. Farmers raised much smaller amounts of food crops and animals. Fresh meat, vegetables, and dairy products were harder to get and more expensive, and many Southerners could no longer afford these nutritious foods. Instead, they ate the cheap 3-M diet.

Whenever the economy slowed and wages dropped, the diet of poorer families deteriorated and pellagra increased.

Another reason the pellagra numbers rose quickly was that physicians became aware of the disease. Before 1906, few American doctors knew anything about pellagra. Once they did, they began to recognize the symptoms in patients.

Who was most likely to die from pellagra?

In the United States, almost 70 percent of all pellagra deaths were women. Mothers in their childbearing years suffered the most. The death rate among blacks was at least six times higher than that among whites. In some years between 1928 and 1940, it was as much as fifteen times higher.

It was not gender or race that made someone more susceptible to pellagra. Except in rare cases, the reason people develop the disease is that they don't take in as much niacin or tryptophan as their bodies need. Women of childbearing age and blacks had higher death rates because they were the most malnourished, had the most advanced stages of pellagra, and were least likely to get medical treatment in time to be saved.

Many women first developed pellagra after having a baby. A woman who is pregnant or nursing needs extra nourishment.

Women in their childbearing years need higher levels of niacin, and they are more likely to develop pellagra if they are malnourished. The young woman has the pellagra rash on her hands and chest.

In addition, when money is short, a mother is more likely to give her share of the expensive foods, such as milk and meat, to her family.

One explanation for the higher death rates among black Southerners is that their diet was even worse than that of poor whites. Another is that they were less likely to get medical care. Finding a doctor to treat them was often difficult. For an impoverished farmer, paying the fee could be impossible.

Why did pellagra appear in spring and early summer?

In the early twentieth century, many Southerners ate meat, milk, eggs, and vegetables only when they were plentiful in the summer and fall. By the end of winter, a family often had eaten all the food stored from the fall harvest. Tenant farmers and sharecroppers also had run out of the cash they earned from the fall crop. In late winter, these families were living on the cheap, less nourishing 3-M diet.

After about six to eight weeks without niacin and tryptophan, a person develops pellagra symptoms. The Public Health Service found that the most common time for new pellagra cases was April through June.

Symptoms usually went away after food crops grew in the summer and farmers received cash from the harvest in the fall. By then, people were eating a better diet again.

The spring appearance of pellagra was also due to the sun. During spring and summer, people spent more hours outside. The sun brought out the dramatic rash in those who had a niacin deficiency. The other symptoms of pellagra, such as digestive problems and nervousness, were often less obvious than the skin changes.

Why does the sun affect the skin that way?

When the body is low in niacin, it doesn't do a good job of repairing skin cells damaged by sun. A normal sunburn turns into a pellagra rash. The intense spring and summer rays do the most damage.

Scientists still don't know the complete answer. Certain chemical changes in the skin may also be part of the explanation.

Are medical experiments on people different today?

One hundred years ago, there were no rules about who could be tested or how the tests should be done. Today, researchers must have informed consent from anyone who agrees to participate in a medical study.

When Joseph Goldberger was searching for pellagra's cause, he took greater care than most researchers to inform his subjects about a test and its possible outcome. In the prison experiment, Goldberger explained to the convicts the dangers of eating a pellagra-causing diet. He encouraged them to talk to their lawyers before volunteering. But by today's rules, this experiment wouldn't be allowed. Because the prisoners were promised their freedom, they might have felt coerced into volunteering.

Physicians have experimented on themselves for centuries, just as Goldberger did in the filth parties. One example is Australian researcher Dr. Barry Marshall, who had a hypothesis that a bacterium caused stomach ulcers. In 1984, he proved it by swallowing a beaker full of the bacteria. Marshall received the 2005 Nobel Prize in Physiology or Medicine for his discovery.

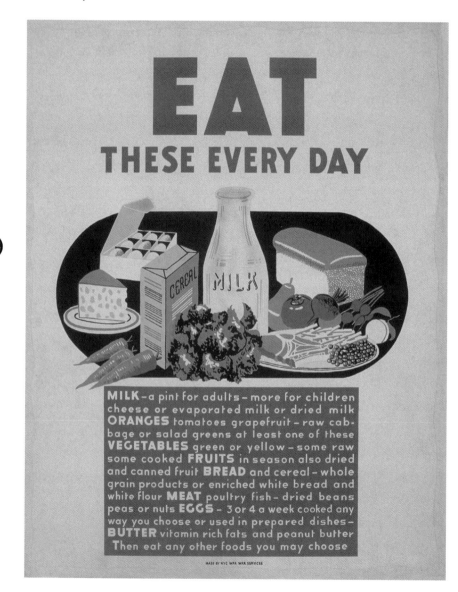

A government poster from World War II reminds Americans to eat a well-balanced diet.

Glossary

Amino acids: the building blocks of proteins.

Arsenic: a poisonous chemical, once thought to be an effective ingredient in medicines, used for a range of illnesses, including pellagra.

Asylum: an institution for the care of mentally ill people; today called a psychiatric hospital.

Bacteria: microscopic one-celled organisms. Some kinds of bacteria are useful, such as those that help break down food in the digestive tract, and others cause disease.

Beriberi: a deficiency disease caused by lack of thiamin (vitamin B_1). Symptoms include weakness or paralysis in the legs, fatigue, and nerve and heart damage.

Biochemistry: the study of the chemistry of life processes in plants and animals.

Black tongue: a deficiency disease in dogs caused by lack of niacin (B_3).

Bubonic plague: a deadly disease caused by a bacterium that is transmitted by fleas. Symptoms include swollen lymph glands, high fever, and seizures.

Communicable disease: a contagious illness that spreads from person to person.

Deficiency disease: an illness caused by the lack of a crucial element in the diet, such as a vitamin or mineral.

Dengue fever: a disease caused by a virus transmitted to humans by mosquitoes. Symptoms include rash, high fever, and muscle and joint pain.

Diphtheria: a contagious disease caused by a bacterium that infects the throat and nose. Symptoms include fever, sore throat, and difficulty breathing. It spreads through droplets from coughs and sneezes and by contaminated objects.

Entomologist: a scientist who studies insects.

Epidemiologist: a medical researcher who investigates the causes of epidemics and the ways to control their spread.

Folic acid: vitamin B$_9$.

Fungi: a group of organisms that get their nourishment from dead or living plants, animals, or other fungi. Examples include molds, mushrooms, and yeasts.

Germ theory: the idea developed during the late nineteenth century that diseases can be caused by microorganisms.

Hookworm: a blood-sucking parasite that lives in the small intestine and causes anemia, weakness, and abdominal pain. It enters the human body through the mouth or skin, usually bare feet that come in contact with infected feces.

Hypothesis: a proposed explanation for an observation, not yet proved by tests or experiments.

Infectious disease: an illness caused by an agent such as a bacterium, virus, or parasite that invades the body.

Laudanum: an opium-based medicine once widely available without a prescription and used to treat pain and a range of illnesses.

Malaria: an infectious disease caused by parasitic microbes transmitted by mosquitoes. Symptoms include fever and chills.

Microorganism (or microbe): a microscopic organism.

Niacin (or nicotinic acid): vitamin B$_3$ or vitamin P-P.

Opium: a drug made from poppies, used in medicine to relieve pain or induce sleep.

Parasite: an animal or plant that benefits from living in, with, or on another organism and often harms its host.

Pellagraphobia: the fear of catching pellagra.

Pellagrin: a person suffering from pellagra.

Quarantine: isolation to prevent contagious diseases or pests from spreading.

Riboflavin: vitamin B$_2$.

Sanitarium: an institution for care of the sick, including the mentally ill. Some sanitariums were once called insane asylums.

Scurvy: a deficiency disease caused by a lack of vitamin C.

Sharecropper: a farmer who arranges to use a landowner's land, tools, work animals, and supplies in return for a portion of the crop he grows.

Smallpox: a contagious disease caused by a virus and spread primarily through face-to-face contact. Symptoms include fever and skin sores.

Strychnine: a poisonous chemical once used in small amounts as a medicine.

Tenant farmer: a farmer who pays rent to a landowner for use of his land.

Theory: an explanation supported by evidence obtained from tests or experiments.

Thiamin: vitamin B_1.

Transfusion: the transfer of blood from a donor into a person's bloodstream.

Tryptophan: an amino acid that people must obtain through their diet because the body cannot produce it.

Tuberculosis: a serious and sometimes fatal infectious lung disease caused by a bacterium spread through the air by coughs and sneezes.

Typhoid fever: an infectious disease caused by a bacterium that spreads through food and water contaminated with feces. Symptoms include high fever, weakness, and abdominal pain.

Typhus: an infectious disease caused by a bacterium that is transmitted by fleas and lice. Symptoms include high fever and red skin rash.

Virus: a minute entity composed of a protein shell containing genetic material that often causes disease when it invades living cells.

Yellow fever: a disease caused by a virus and spread by mosquitoes. Symptoms include fever, vomiting, and body aches.

Timeline

1735   First written account of pellagra, in Spain.

1861–65   American Civil War.

1874   July 16—Joseph Goldberger born in Giralt, Austro-Hungarian Empire.

1883   November—Goldberger immigrates to the United States with his family.

1899   Goldberger joins the Public Health Service.

1902   H. F. Harris is first to report pellagra in America, in Georgia.

1906   George Searcy observes pellagra outbreak at an Alabama insane hospital.

1908   Public Health Service begins to study pellagra.

1909   November—First meeting of the National Association for the Study of Pellagra, in Columbia, South Carolina.

1911   Illinois Pellagra Commission concludes that pellagra is caused by a microbe.

1912   Casimir Funk suggests pellagra might be a deficiency disease.

            October—Second meeting of the National Association for the Study of Pellagra.

1912–13   Thompson-McFadden Pellagra Commission concludes that pellagra is an infectious disease.

1914   February—Goldberger put in charge of Public Health Service's pellagra investigation.

            June—Goldberger announces that a deficient diet may cause pellagra.

            July—World War I breaks out in Europe.

1914–15   Goldberger tests his hypothesis in orphanages, a mental asylum, and a prison.

1916   Goldberger holds his filth parties and conducts mill-village study.

1917–18	U.S. fights in World War I.
1918–29	Goldberger searches for the pellagra-preventing substance in foods.
1920	Cotton prices plummet.
1927	Great Mississippi River Flood. Red Cross distributes yeast to prevent and cure pellagra.
1929	January 17—Joseph Goldberger dies. Great Depression begins.
1937	Conrad Elvehjem discovers that factor P-P is nicotinic acid.
1938	Commercial bakers voluntarily enrich bread with yeast.
1939	World War II begins in Europe.
1941	May—National Nutrition Conference for the Defense recommends bread and flour enrichment. December—U.S. enters World War II.
1943	January—Federal war order requires enrichment of commercially baked white bread.
1945	August—World War II ends.
1946	Wartime enrichment order is lifted. Most bakeries continue to fortify bread.

For More Information*

ON PELLAGRA

Pellagra.
PBS LearningMedia, PBS & WGBH Educational Foundation.
pbslearningmedia.org/search/?q=pellagra
　　Watch a five-minute video on Joseph Goldberger's pellagra research. Site includes discussion questions and curriculum links to state standards and the Common Core.

"Pellagra and Its Prevention and Control in Major Emergencies." Nutrition in Emergencies.
World Health Organization (WHO), 2000.
who.int/topics/nutrition/publications/emergencies/en
　　Scroll down for the pdf on pellagra. The article includes an overview of the disease, its symptoms, current medical treatments, and recent outbreaks.

Public Health Reports (1896–1970).
U.S. National Library of Medicine,
National Institutes of Health.
ncbi.nlm.nih.gov/pmc/journals/347/#pubhealthreporig
　　Read the original reports about the pellagra investigation written by Public Health Service officers, including Joseph Goldberger. The journal is searchable.

ON JOSEPH GOLDBERGER

"Dr. Joseph Goldberger and the War on Pellagra"
by Alan M. Kraut.
Office of NIH History.
history.nih.gov/exhibits/Goldberger
　　View an online exhibit about Goldberger's life. Includes photographs.

*Websites active at time of publication

Goldberger's War: The Life and Work of a Public Health Crusader by Alan M. Kraut. New York: Hill and Wang, 2003.

This book, written by a historian at American University, is the most recent biography of Goldberger. Previous biographies were published in 1928 (de Kruif) and 1943 (Parsons) and are listed in the bibliography.

"Joseph Goldberger" by W. H. Sebrell.
The Journal of Nutrition, January 1, 1955.
jn.nutrition.org/content/55/1/1.full.pdf+html

The biographical article was written by one of Goldberger's assistants who later served as director of the National Institutes of Health from 1950 to 1955.

ON PUBLIC HEALTH AND DISEASE

Centers for Disease Control and Prevention (CDC).
cdc.gov

This site contains information on diseases, healthy living, injury and safety, and many other public health topics. Find weekly reports on disease outbreaks by state in the "Morbidity and Mortality Weekly Report" (MMWR) at cdc.gov/mmwr.

United States Public Health Service (USPHS).
usphs.gov

Learn about the mission of the PHS and the opportunities for a career in public health.

ON NUTRITION

BAM! Body and Mind.
Centers for Disease Control and Prevention.
bam.gov

This interactive website for teens includes information about food, nutrition, diseases, safety, and physical activity. Play the online games and try the recipes for healthy treats.

"Dietary Guidelines for Americans."
U.S. Departments of Agriculture and Health and Human Services.
health.gov/dietaryguidelines

This site includes lists of vitamin, nutrient, and calorie content of foods. Read the government's recommendations for improving diet, and follow links to other resources on nutrition and physical activity.

Nutrition Information for You.
U.S. Department of Agriculture.
nutrition.gov

In the "What's in Food" section, find out everything you want to know about your food, including nutrients, vitamins, and additives. Learn which foods have the highest niacin content. The "Life Stages: Adolescents" section is designed especially for teens.

ON SOUTHERN COTTON MILL WORKERS AND FARMERS

Prints & Photographs Online Catalog. Library of Congress.
loc.gov/pictures

Search by "mill worker," "cotton mills," "sharecropper," or "tenant farmer" to view thousands of photographs of the American South during the early twentieth century.

ON THE 1927 MISSISSIPPI RIVER FLOOD

Mississippi River Flood of 1927.
Internet Archive.
archive.org/details/mississippi_flood_1927

Watch a seventeen-minute silent film produced by the U.S. Signal Corps. The film shows the devastation, the frantic attempts to hold back the water, the evacuation of farm animals, the rescue of people from rooftops, and the makeshift camps for refugees, who were separated by race.

"1927 Flood Photograph Collection."
Mississippi Department of Archives and History.
mdah.state.ms.us/arrec/digital_archives/1927flood

    See dozens of photographs taken in April, May, and October of 1927 showing the flood damage from Tennessee through Louisiana.

An Arkansas house is submerged during the 1927 Mississippi River flood.

163

Author's Note

The first time I read about pellagra was in the Cornell University Library stacks when I was researching scurvy for a magazine article. A yellow-covered book, *A Plague of Corn: The Social History of Pellagra*, caught my eye. A few years earlier, I had met the author, Daphne A. Roe, a local dermatologist and Cornell professor of nutritional sciences. Fascinated by her story about this nearly forgotten disease, I filed away my notes on her book.

It took me a dozen years to pull them out again and start *Red Madness*. I'm glad I waited. During that period, advances in online databases and search engines made it possible for me to explore materials I couldn't access twelve years earlier. Now I was able to hunt for information and images in national and international library collections, medical journals, and hundreds of newspapers.

I planned to write my book as a medical detective story. I already knew the surprise ending from reading Roe's book and another excellent overview, *The Butterfly Caste: A Social History of Pellagra in the South* by historian Elizabeth W. Etheridge. But I wanted to experience for myself the twists and turns, errors, and confusion that marked the investigation into pellagra's cause and cure. I decided to carry out my research the way history unfolded, starting with the first report of pellagra in the United States in 1902.

What did physicians and scientists of the early 1900s know about pellagra? What did they believe was its cause? I found the answers in their own words published in medical journals, books, and the reports of several pellagra commissions.

What was it like to have pellagra? In the Waring Historical Library at the Medical University of South Carolina in Charleston, I combed through personal notebooks, scrapbooks, doctors' reports, and victims' photographs collected by the early pellagra fighter Dr. James Babcock. I learned about individual patients and their physicians' attempts to cure them.

Checking Southern newspapers and magazines published a hundred years ago, I uncovered dozens of articles about pellagra sufferers. In the Southern Oral History Program Collection at the University of North Carolina-Chapel Hill, I located interviews with pellagra victims. These tragic stories helped me understand why doctors and scientists tried so desperately to stop the pellagra epidemic.

In the Library of Congress, I found photographs of sharecroppers and mill workers, two groups who suffered the most from the disease. The images showed me the people behind the statistics: farm families toiling under a hot summer sun, small children carrying bags of cotton almost as heavy as they were, a tired and haggard young mother sitting on the porch of a run-down mill-village house.

When my research brought me to 1914, medical sleuth Joseph Goldberger took the stage. I read about his life in three biographies. The 1928 book *Hunger Fighters* by biologist and journalist Paul de Kruif contains an account based on de Kruif's interviews with Goldberger shortly before the doctor's death.

Trail to Light: A Biography of Joseph Goldberger, published in 1943, was written by former Naval doctor Robert P. Parsons, who had met Goldberger during the influenza epidemic of 1918. Mary Goldberger let Parsons look through thousands of personal letters, notebooks, and scrapbooks, and he interviewed her as well as many family members and friends.

In 2003, historian Alan M. Kraut of American University expanded on these two earlier accounts in *Goldberger's War: The Life and Work of a Public Health Crusader*. Kraut added information and insight based on his exploration of historical documents and his interviews with Goldberger's son and others.

To get my own close-up view of Goldberger, I immersed myself in his personal correspondence stored in the Southern Historical Collection at the University of North Carolina-Chapel Hill. These papers include Goldberger's handwritten letters to Mary, sent while he sought pellagra's cause and cure. Because these were intimate and private, they reveal Goldberger's unguarded opinions about his work and the people around him.

I also read his public writings to find out—from his own explanations—how he tackled and eventually cracked the case. Goldberger investigated pellagra for fifteen years, and his many scientific papers appeared in *Public Health Reports*, which are available online. More than a dozen papers are also printed in *Goldberger on Pellagra*, edited by Milton Terris.

In seeking another perspective on Goldberger, I read criticisms of his work, many of which appeared in *Southern Medical Journal*. These attacks on his ideas show the reluctance of Southern physicians to acknowledge the connection between their region's economy, diet, and disease.

As I approached the final solution of the pellagra mystery, I examined the scientific papers announcing the effect of nicotinic acid on pellagra victims. In checking twenty-first-century medical literature, I discovered that researchers continue to work toward a more complete understanding of the biochemistry and physiology of the disease.

To get answers to my remaining questions about pellagra, I interviewed experts in medicine, nutritional science, and history.

Looking back at a century of pellagra history, I am reminded of the importance of following the scientific method. If every researcher and physician who studied pellagra had done that, the disease might have been conquered long before Joseph Goldberger came along.

Unfortunately, some of them made the mistake of assuming that since pellagra was *associated* with corn eaters, corn *caused* pellagra. Others missed critical clues because they didn't make careful observations, and this led them to flawed hypotheses. Instead of keeping an open mind when they analyzed the results of tests and experiments, they ignored facts and evidence that contradicted their pet hypotheses.

While pellagra researchers headed in the wrong direction, millions of people suffered.

Source Notes

The source of each quotation in this book is found below. The citation indicates the first words of the quotation and its document source. The document sources are listed either in the bibliography or below.

CHAPTER ONE, page 6

"An Awful . . .": "The Pellagra," *New York Times*, November 9, 1879.

"unfit for . . .": Searcy, p. 37.

"especially in the south . . .": same as above, p. 38.

"swallowing live . . .": quoted in Carter, p. 100.

"a very large eater . . ." and "defective": "Pellagra Case at Newberry," *Columbus Enquirer-Sun*, October 22, 1908.

"Pellagra Found . . .": *State*, January 15, 1908.

"South Menaced . . .": same as above, January 31, 1909.

"Dying of a . . .": *Kansas City Times*, October 10, 1908.

"The disease has . . .": C. H. Lavinder, "The Prophylaxis of Pellagra," *Public Health Reports*, October 29, 1909, pp. 1618–19.

"not only very severe . . .": Francesco Frapolli, "Observations upon a Disease Commonly Called Pelagra," translated by C. H. Lavinder, Babcock Papers.

CHAPTER TWO, page 22

"The more you . . .": J. W. Babcock, quoted in Carter, p. 104.

"prominent girl" and "that rare . . .": "Prominent Girl Is Victim of Pellagra," *Columbus Enquirer-Sun*, October 10, 1908.

"the strange . . .": "Death from Pellagra," *Biloxi Daily Herald*, October 10, 1908.

"We are menaced . . .": Geo. A. Zeller, *National Conference on Pellagra*, p. 52.

"I have had extensive . . .": J. J. Watson, same as above, p. 194.

"If there is any . . .": Hiram Byrd, same as above.

"It attacked . . .": "Death from Pellagra," *Biloxi Daily Herald*, April 29, 1909.

"There is a new . . .": "Terrible New Disease," *Adair County News*, November 10, 1909.

"Incurable Pellagra" and "Musty cornmeal . . .": "This Mother and Her Whole Brood Suffer from Incurable Pellagra," *Wilkes-Barre Times-Leader*, May 19, 1910.

"If You Fear . . .": *New York Times*, September 5, 1909.

"We of the South . . .": *Wilmington Star*, quoted in "The Pellagra Problem," *Columbia Daily Record*, November 8, 1909.

"I have fought . . .": quoted in Wood, p. 268.

"I'm scared . . .": quoted in W. F. Lorenz, "Mental Manifestations of Pellagra," *Public Health Reports*, February 4, 1916, p. 229.

"blew her brains . . .": "Suffering from Pellagra Woman Commits Suicide," *Biloxi Daily Herald*, April 14, 1911.

CHAPTER THREE, page 36

"In the history . . .": Claude H. Lavinder, "The Prophylaxis of Pellagra," *Public Health Reports*, October 29, 1909, p. 1621.

"A National Calamity": *Annual Report of the Surgeon General*, 1912, p. 32.

"In many sections . . .": same as above.

"Pellagra . . .": Grimm, *Public Health Reports*, March 14, 1913, p. 512.

"the richest . . .": "Richest Indian Child," *Biloxi Daily Herald*, August 16, 1911.

"may so alter . . .": Illinois Pellagra Commission, p. 249.

"well-nourished . . .": Siler, *Pellagra II*, p. 90.

"extremely fond . . .": Roy Blosser, "Some Observations Further Incriminating Sugar-Cane Products as the Main Cause of Pellagra in the South," *Southern Medical Journal*, January 1915, pp. 33–34.

"If the cause . . .": *National Association for the Study of Pellagra*, p. 2.

CHAPTER FOUR, page 50

"The disease appears . . .": Garman, p. 11.

"who have been swarming . . .": René Bache, "Pellagra Caused by Gnat?", *Technical World Magazine*, August 1910, p. 652.

"There is a suggestion . . .": "Beware of Pellagra," *Washington Post*, August 23, 1909.

"Wife of Railroad . . .": "First Pellagra Case Fatal," *Fort Worth Star-Telegram*, November 23, 1909.

"inherited vitality": Bernard Wolff, "Are the Jews Immune to Pellagra?", *Southern Medical Journal*, March 1912, p. 124.

"It occurs more . . .": U. L. Taylor, "A Timely Warning," *Adair County News*, July 27, 1910.

"poor, overworked . . .": Grimm, *Public Health Reports*, March 7, 1913, p. 441.

"lived out of . . .": quoted in Grimm, same as above, p. 445.

"the relationship . . .": Grimm, *Public Health Reports*, March 14, 1913, p. 513.

"The disease is not confined . . .": Wood, p. 131.

"Pellagra Robs . . .": *Fort Worth Star-Telegram*, July 9, 1913.

"a patient suffering . . .": James M. King, "The Treatment of Pellagra," *International Clinics*, 1910, vol. 1, series 20, p. 58.

"Owing to the possibility . . .": Deaderick, p. 382.

"because the disease . . .": "Pellagra Patients Create a Problem," *Columbus Enquirer-Sun*, December 20, 1914.

"Beware of . . .": *Washington Post*, August 23, 1909.

"it is a disease . . .": U. L. Taylor, "A Timely Warning," *Adair County News*, July 27, 1910.

"Please tell me . . .": Wood, p. 274.

"corn-bread . . .": H. F. Harris, quoted in Niles, p. 76.

"the best treatment . . .": "Uses the Appendix to 'Cure' Pellagra," *Fort Worth Star-Telegram*, December 11, 1910.

"a young person . . .": "Anyone Got Any Blood for Sale?" *Fort Worth Star-Telegram*, April 27, 1911.

"Cured of Pellagra . . .": *Macon Daily Telegraph*, July 2, 1915.

"Have you pains . . .": and "the MAD HOUSE . . ." and "grim specter . . .": quoted in "Baughn's Pellagra Remedy, A Worthless Nostrum Sold Under Fraudulent Claims," *Journal of the American Medical Association*, November 15, 1913, p. 1828.

"Nausea . . .": quoted in "Pellagracide and EZ-X-BA, Fraudulent Nostrums Sold as Cures of Pellagra," *Journal of the American Medical Association*, March 2, 1912, p. 648.

"On my darker . . .": quoted in Wood, p. 274.

"My sufferings . . .": quoted in "Pellagra Victim Drowns Self in Thirty-Foot Well," *Macon Daily Telegraph*, June 6, 1913.

CHAPTER FIVE, page 64

"You are preeminently . . .": letter from Rupert Blue to Goldberger, February 7, 1914, Goldberger Papers, box 2.

"one of the knottiest . . .": same as above.

"This is childish . . .": Goldberger, quoted in Parsons, p. 223.

"Of course I wrote . . .": letter from Goldberger to Mary Goldberger, February 9, 1914, Goldberger Papers, box 2.

"Her death is . . .": "Miss Maud Johnson," *State*, February 7, 1914.

CHAPTER SIX, page 78

"I hope that in due . . .": letter from Goldberger to Mary
      Goldberger, September 17, 1914, Goldberger Papers, box 2.

"If pellagra . . .": Joseph Goldberger, "The Etiology of
      Pellagra," *Public Health Reports*, June 26, 1914, p. 1684.

"the light of battle . . .": Mary Goldberger, "Science
      Pigeonholed—Pellagra," Goldberger Papers, box 3.

"She was shocked . . .": Death Notice, *Lexington Herald*,
      April 24, 1914.

"to prevent . . .": Joseph Goldberger, "The Etiology of
      Pellagra," *Public Health Reports*, June 26, 1914, p. 1686.

"The poor, helpless . . .": letter from Goldberger to Mary
      Goldberger, October 3, 1914, Goldberger Papers, box 2.

"Are you all . . ." and "Oh! . . .": quoted in above.

"They are all . . .": same as above, June 20, 1915.

"We surely can . . ." and "The work . . .": same as above.

"My inferences . . .": same as above, April 25, 1915.

"It almost seems . . .": same as above, June 24, 1915.

"The results clearly . . .": same as above, October 30, 1915.

"I have been begging . . .": J. W. Pope, quoted in "Pope Tells a
      Pitiful Story," *Columbus Ledger*, May 2, 1915.

"I need hardly tell . . .": letter from Goldberger to Mary
      Goldberger, October 30, 1915, Goldberger Papers, box 2.

"like a lot of scared . . .": same as above, November 2, 1915.

"I have been through . . ." and "He said to eat . . .": quoted in
      "Tortured by Pellagra," *Washington Post*,
      November 7, 1915.

"Nothing is certain . . .": letter from Goldberger to Mary
      Goldberger, July 3, 1915, Goldberger Papers, box 2.

"Abundance of Protein . . .": "Supposed Cure Found for
      Pellagra," *New York Times*, November 12, 1915.

"Pellagra Cure . . .": *Washington Post*, November 12, 1915.

"The Southern states . . .": Hendrick, p. 639.

"'Diet' wins . . .": letter from Goldberger to Mary
    Goldberger, October 23, 1915, Goldberger Papers, box 2.

"I'm just as pleased . . .": same as above, November 25, 1915.

"to turn on . . .": same as above, September 17, 1914.

CHAPTER SEVEN, page 96

"[They] swallowed . . .": Mary Farrar Goldberger, *Essays*,
    p. 286.

"would have proved . . .": Deaderick, p. 301.

"flatter themselves . . .": letter from Goldberger to Mary
    Goldberger, November 19, 1914, Goldberger Papers,
    box 2.

"former patients . . .": same as above, December 19, 1914.

"Most pellagra patients . . .": B. H. Booth, quoted in "Wide
    Divergence About Pellagra," *State*, November 17, 1915.

"I want to enter . . .": J. L. Jelks, same as above.

"blind, selfish . . .": letter from Goldberger to Mary
    Goldberger, November 25, 1915, Goldberger Papers,
    box 2.

"to the plain . . .": same as above, April 25, 1915.

"We've been giving . . .": Goldberger, quoted in "'We
    Starve 50,000 People a Year and Call It Pellagra!'",
    Wilkes-Barre Times-Leader, November 12, 1915.

"I can not emphasize . . .": Goldberger, quoted in "Use
    Dieting Plan to Cure Pellagra," *State*, August 28, 1915.

"I begged . . .": Mary Farrar Goldberger, *Essays*, p. 286.

"filth party": letter from Goldberger to Mary Goldberger,
    June 25, 1916, Goldberger Papers, box 2.

"We had our final . . .": same as above.

"When one considers . . .": Joseph Goldberger, "The
    Transmissibility of Pellagra," *Public Health Reports*,
    November 17, 1916, p. 3166.

"The pitiful . . .": letter from Goldberger to Mary Goldberger,
    March 25, 1917, Goldberger Papers, box 2.

"The single-crop . . .": Joseph Goldberger, G. A. Wheeler, and Edgar Sydenstricker, "A Study of the Relation of Family Income and Other Economic Factors to Pellagra Incidence in Seven Cotton-Mill Villages of South Carolina in 1916," *Public Health Reports*, November 12, 1920, p. 2711.

"There are many . . .": letter from Goldberger to Mary Goldberger, May 20, 1917, Goldberger Papers, box 2.

"If all people . . .": Joseph Goldberger, "Pellagra, Its Nature and Prevention," *Public Health Reports*, April 5, 1918, p. 488.

"Own a cow": quoted in "Will Discontinue Pellagra Hospital," *State*, July 19, 1920.

"ignorant . . .": G. A. Wheeler, "Pellagra in the Mountains of Yancey County, North Carolina," *Public Health Reports*, October 22, 1920, p. 2514.

CHAPTER EIGHT, page 114

"It is the poor man . . .": Joseph Goldberger, "Pellagra, Its Nature and Prevention," *Public Health Reports*, April 5, 1918, p. 484.

"Pellagra has practically . . .": "Will Discontinue Pellagra Hospital," *State*, July 19, 1920.

"to save the lives . . .": quoted in "Plague Threatens 100,000 Victims in the Cotton Belt," *New York Times*, July 25, 1921.

"It must bring . . .": Warren G. Harding, quoted in "Orders Relief for Pellagra Victims," *New York Times*, July 26, 1921.

"The average American . . .": James Byrnes, quoted in "Wants Refutation of Pellagra Scare," *New York Times*, July 31, 1921.

"The South is . . .": Thomas J. Hamilton, editor, *Augusta Chronicle*, quoted in "South Resents Federal Alarm Over Pellagra, Exaggerated, Says Georgia," *New York Times*, July 27, 1921.

"propaganda": Harris, *Clinical Pellagra*, p. 398.

"slander": same as above, p. 397.

"I'm only a . . .": de Kruif, pp. 362–63.

"floods of saliva . . .": Baxter Haynes, "Pellagra from the Viewpoint of the Patient," *International Clinics*, 1926, vol. 4, series 36, p. 76.

"eat it . . .": same as above, p. 78.

"we desired . . .": Joseph Goldberger and G. A. Wheeler, "Experimental Black Tongue of Dogs and Its Relation to Pellagra," *Public Health Reports*, January 27, 1928, p. 176.

"Dear Doctor . . .": letter from Mrs. E. C. Belisle to Joseph Goldberger, March 31, 1925, Goldberger Papers, box 2.

"It burned . . ." and "'Don't worry . . .'" and "they found . . .": Jessie Lee Carter, interviewed by Allen Tullos, May 5, 1980, Southern Oral History Program Collection.

"The problem . . .": Joseph Goldberger, *Essays*, p. 106.

"beyond reasonable . . .": same as above, p. 104.

"one of the . . .": Surgeon General Cumming, quoted in "Dr. Goldberger Dies Martyr to Science," *New York Times*, January 18, 1929.

"keen, scientific . . .": "Dr. Goldberger Dies Martyr to Science," same as above.

"I know what . . .": Joseph Goldberger, quoted by Mary Farrar Goldberger, *Essays*, p. 287.

CHAPTER NINE, page 132

"An ailment . . .": "Conquest of Pellagra," *New York Times*, June 19, 1938.

"Its [nicotinic acid] . . .": letter from Tom D. Spies to Mary Goldberger, December 16, 1938, Goldberger Papers, box 3.

"one of the most horrible . . .": "Pellagra Victim Shown to Doctors," *New York Times*, December 17, 1909.

Bibliography

Akin, C. V. *Control of Pellagra: A Community Problem and a Public Responsibility*. Columbia: South Carolina State Board of Health, 1932.

Annual Report of the Surgeon General of the Public Health Service of the United States for the Fiscal Year 1912. Washington, DC: Government Printing Office, 1913, 31–33.

Babcock, James Woods. Papers. Waring Historical Library, Medical University of South Carolina, Charleston.

————. "Prevalence of Pellagra." Article reprinted from the *Journal of the South Carolina Medical Association, September 1910*. Washington, DC: Government Printing Office, 1911.

Billings, Frank, and J. H. Salisbury, eds. *General Medicine* (The Practical Medicine Series), series 1912, vol. 6: 69–82.

Bollet, Alfred Jay. *Plagues & Poxes: The Impact of Human History on Epidemic Disease*. 2nd ed. New York: Demos Medical Publishing, 2004.

The Campaign Against Malnutrition. Public Health Bulletin No. 134. Washington, DC: Treasury Department, United States Public Health Service, 1923.

Carpenter, Kenneth J., ed. *Pellagra*. Stroudsburg, PA: Hutchinson Ross Publishing, 1981.

————. "A Short History of Nutritional Science: Part 3 (1912–1944)." *Journal of Nutrition*, October 2003: 3023–32.

————. "A Short History of Nutritional Science: Part 4 (1945–1985)." *Journal of Nutrition*, November 2003: 3331–42.

Carter, Mary Hamilton. "Pellagra, The Medical Mystery of To-Day." *McClure's Magazine*, November 1909: 94–107.

"Corn and Pellagra." *American Review of Reviews*. Edited by Albert Shaw. January–June 1910: 351–52.

Daniel, Pete. *Breaking the Land: The Transformation of Cotton, Tobacco, and Rice Cultures since 1880*. Urbana: University of Illinois Press, 1985.

Davenport, Charles B. "The Hereditary Factor in Pellagra." *Eugenics Record Office*, July 1916, Bulletin No. 16, 1–29. Reprinted from *Archives of Internal Medicine*, vol. 18.

Deaderick, William H., and Loyd Thompson. *The Endemic Diseases of the Southern States*. Philadelphia: W. B. Saunders, 1916.

de Kruif, Paul. *Hunger Fighters*. New York: Harcourt Brace, 1928.

Ebrahim, G. J. "Problems of Undernutrition." In *Nutrition and Disease*. Edited by R. J. Jarrett. Baltimore: University Park Press, 1979.

Elvehjem, Conrad A. "A Forty-Year Look at Nutrition Research." In *Essays on History of Nutrition and Dietetics*. Compiled by Adelia M. Beeuwkes, E. Neige Todhunter, and Emma Seifrit Weigley. Chicago: American Dietetic Association, 1967.

Etheridge, Elizabeth W. *The Butterfly Caste: A Social History of Pellagra in the South*. Westport, CT: Greenwood Publishing, 1972.

_____. "Pellagra: An Unappreciated Reminder of Southern Distinctiveness." In *Disease and Distinctiveness in the American South*. Edited by Todd L. Savitt and James Harvey Young. Knoxville: University of Tennessee Press, 1988.

Frankenburg, Frances Rachel. *Vitamin Discoveries and Disasters: History, Science, and Controversies*. Santa Barbara, CA: Praeger, 2009.

French, Herbert. *An Index of Differential Diagnosis of Main Symptoms*. 3rd ed. New York: William Wood and Company, 1917.

Funk, Casimir. "The Etiology of the Deficiency Diseases: Beri-Beri, Polyneuritis in Birds, Epidemic Dropsy, Scurvy-Experimental, Scurvy in Animals, Infantile Scurvy, Ship Beri-Beri, Pellagra." *Journal of State Medicine*, June 1912: 341–63.

Furman, Bess. *A Profile of the United States Public Health Service, 1798–1948*. Washington, DC: U.S. Department of Health, Education, and Welfare; National Institutes of Health; and National Library of Medicine, 1973.

Garman, H. *A Preliminary Study of Kentucky Localities in Which Pellagra Is Prevalent*. Lexington: Kentucky Agricultural Experiment Station of the State University, 1912.

Goldberger, Joseph. *Goldberger on Pellagra*. Edited by Milton Terris. Baton Rouge: Louisiana State University Press, 1964.

_____. Papers. #1641. Southern Historical Collection, Wilson Library, University of North Carolina at Chapel Hill.

_____. "Pellagra." In *Essays on History of Nutrition and Dietetics*. Compiled by Adelia M. Beeuwkes, E. Neige Todhunter, and Emma Seifrit Weigley. Chicago: American Dietetic Association, 1967.

Goldberger, Mary Farrar. "Dr. Joseph Goldberger, His Wife's Recollections." In *Essays on History of Nutrition and Dietetics*. Compiled by Adelia M. Beeuwkes, E. Neige Todhunter, and Emma Seifrit Weigley. Chicago: American Dietetic Association, 1967.

Grimm, R. M. "Pellagra: A Report on Its Epidemiology." *Public Health Reports*, March 7, 1913: 427–50, and March 14, 1913: 491–513.

Hall, Jacquelyn Dowd, and James Leloudis, Robert Korstad, Mary Murphy, Lu Ann Jones, Christopher B. Daly. *Like a Family: The Making of a Southern Cotton Mill World*. Chapel Hill: University of North Carolina Press, 2000.

Harkness, Jon M. "Prisoners and Pellagra." *Public Health Reports*, September–October 1996: 463–67.

Harris, H. F. "A Case of Ankylostomiasis Presenting the Symptoms of Pellagra." *Transactions of the Medical Association of Georgia*, 1902: 220–27.

_____. *Pellagra*. New York: Macmillan, 1919.

Harris, Seale. *Clinical Pellagra*. St. Louis: C. V. Mosby, 1941.

Hegyi, Juraj, Robert A. Schwartz, and Vladmir Hegyi. "Pellagra: Dermatitis, Dementia, and Diarrhea." *International Journal of Dermatology*, January 2004: 1–5.

Hendrick, Burton J. "The Mastery of Pellagra." *World's Work*, April 1916: 633–39.

Humphreys, Margaret. "How Four Once Common Diseases Were Eliminated from the American South." *Health Affairs*, November–December 2009: 1734–44.

Illinois Pellagra Commission. *Report of the Pellagra Commission of the State of Illinois, November, 1911*. Springfield: Illinois State Journal Company, 1912.

Jukes, Thomas H. "Tom Douglas Spies." *Journal of Nutrition*, November 1, 1972: 1395–1400.

Karthikeyan, Kaliaperumal, and Devinder Mohan Thappa. "Pellagra and Skin." *International Journal of Dermatology*, 2002, vol. 41: 476–81.

Kraut, Alan M. *Goldberger's War: The Life and Work of a Public Health Crusader*. New York: Hill and Wang, 2003.

Kunitz, Stephen J. "Hookworm and Pellagra: Exemplary Diseases in the New South." *Journal of Health and Social Behavior*, June 1988: 139–48.

Lavinder, C. H. *Pellagra: A Précis*. Washington, DC: Government Printing Office, 1908.

_____."The Prevalence and Geographic Distribution of Pellagra in the United States." *Public Health Reports*, December 13, 1912: 2076–88.

_____."The Prevalence of Pellagra in the United States—A Statistical and Geographical Note, with Bibliography." *Public Health Reports*, June 18, 1909: 849–52.

Leslie, Chris. "'Fighting an Unseen Enemy': The Infectious Paradigm in the Conquest of Pellagra." *Journal of Medical Humanities*, Winter 2002: 187–202.

Marie, Armand. *Pellagra*. Translated and adapted by C. H. Lavinder and J. W. Babcock. Columbia, SC: State Company, 1910.

Marks, Harry M. "Epidemiologists Explain Pellagra: Gender, Race, and Political Economy in the Work of Edgar Sydenstricker." *Journal of the History of Medicine and Allied Sciences*, January 2003: 34–55.

Miller, Donald F. "Cereal Enrichment/Pellagra—USA . . . In Perspective 1977." Address presented at Annual Meeting, American Association of Cereal Chemists, October 24, 1977.

Mullan, Fitzhugh. *Plagues and Politics: The Story of the United States Public Health Service*. New York: Basic Books, 1989.

National Association for the Study of Pellagra, Second Triennial Meeting, October 3 and 4, 1912. Transactions. Columbia, SC: R. L. Bryan, 1914.

National Conference on Pellagra Held Under Auspices of South Carolina State Board of Health, November 3 and 4, 1909. Transactions. Columbia, SC: State Company, 1910.

Niles, George M. *Pellagra: An American Problem*. Philadelphia: W. B. Saunders, 1912.

Park, Youngmee K., Christopher T. Sempos, Curtis N. Barton, John E. Vanderveen, and Elizabeth A. Yetley. "Effectiveness of Food Fortification in the United States: The Case of Pellagra." *American Journal of Public Health*, May 2000: 727–38.

Parsons, Robert P. *Trail to Light: A Biography of Joseph Goldberger*. Indianapolis: Bobbs-Merrill, 1943.

*Pellagra: A Report Upon 316 Cases of This Disease as
Submitted by the Commission Appointed by the Tennessee
State Board of Health*. Nashville: Tennessee Pellagra
Commission, 1911.

Potwin, Marjorie A. *Cotton Mill People of the Piedmont:
A Study in Social Change*. New York: Columbia
University Press, 1927.

Prinzo, Zita Weise. *Pellagra and Its Prevention and Control
in Major Emergencies*. Geneva: Department of Nutrition
and Development, World Health Organization, 2000.

Rajakumar, Kumaravel. "Pellagra in the United States:
A Historical Perspective." *Southern Medical Journal*,
March 2000: 272–77.

Rhyne, Jennings J. *Some Southern Cotton Mill Workers and
Their Villages*. Chapel Hill, NC: University of North
Carolina Press, 1930.

Roberts, Stewart R. *Pellagra: History, Distribution, Diagnosis,
Prognosis, Treatment, Etiology*. St. Louis: C. V. Mosby,
1912.

Roe, Daphne A. *A Plague of Corn: The Social History of
Pellagra*. Ithaca, NY: Cornell University Press, 1973.

Searcy, George H. "An Epidemic of Acute Pellagra."
Journal of the American Medical Association,
July 6, 1907: 37–38.

Sebrell, W. H. "Joseph Goldberger." *Journal of Nutrition*,
January 1, 1955: 1–12.

Siler, J. F., P. E. Garrison, and W. J. MacNeal. *Pellagra:
First Progress Report of the Thompson-McFadden
Pellagra Commission*. New York: New York Post
Graduate Medical School and Hospital, 1913.

_____. *Pellagra II: Second Progress Report of the Thompson
McFadden Pellagra Commission*. New York:
New York Post-Graduate Medical School and Hospital,
1914.

Sledge, Daniel Davis. "Southern Maladies: Politics and Public Health in the Pre-Civil Rights South, 1902–1950." PhD diss., Cornell University, 2010.

Southern Oral History Program Collection, Documenting the American South, University Library, University of North Carolina at Chapel Hill.

Spies, Tom D. *Rehabilitation Through Better Nutrition*. Philadelphia: W. B. Saunders, 1947.

Spies, Tom D., Clark Cooper, and M. A. Blankenhorn. "The Use of Nicotinic Acid in the Treatment of Pellagra." *Journal of the American Medical Association*, February 26, 1938: 622–27.

A Statistical Report of Pellagra in Mississippi and Suggestions to the Legislature Relative to Its Prevention and Cure. Jackson: State of Mississippi Board of Health, 1915.

Sydenstricker, V. P. "The History of Pellagra, Its Recognition as a Disorder of Nutrition and Its Conquest." *American Journal of Clinical Nutrition*, July–August 1958: 409–14.

Watson, J. J. "Symptomatology of Pellagra." *International Clinics*, 1910, vol. 1, series 20: 42–57.

Wheeler, G. A. "A Note on the History of Pellagra in the United States." *Public Health Reports*, September 18, 1931: 2223–29.

Wilder, Russell M. "A Brief History of the Enrichment of Flour and Bread." *Journal of the American Medical Association*, December 22, 1956: 1539–41.

Wood, Edward Jenner. *A Treatise on Pellagra for the General Practitioner*. New York: D. Appleton, 1912.

Zeller, George A. "Pellagra: Some Clinical and Other Features of the Disease." Reprint from *Interstate Medical Journal*, vol. 17, no. 10. St Louis: Interstate Medical Journal Company, 1910.

_____. "The Spread of Pellagra Throughout the United States." *International Clinics*, 1911, vol. 1, series 21: 1–9.

The following periodicals:

Adair [KY] *County News*

American Journal of Public Health

Biloxi [MS] *Daily Herald*

Charlotte [NC] *Daily Observer*

Columbia [SC] *Daily Record*

Columbus [GA] *Enquirer-Sun*

Columbus [GA] *Ledger*

Dallas [TX] *Morning News*

Duluth [MN] *News Tribune*

Fort Worth [TX] *Star-Telegram*

International Clinics

Journal of the American Medical Association

Journal of Nutrition

Journal of the South Carolina Medical Association

Kansas City [MO] *Times*

Lexington [KY] *Herald*

Macon [GA] *Daily Telegraph*

New York Times

Public Health Reports

Southern Medical Journal

State [Columbia, SC]

Technical World Magazine

Time magazine

Washington Post

Wilkes-Barre [PA] *Times-Leader*

Wilmington [NC] *Star*

Index

*Page numbers in **boldface** refer to images and/or captions.*

Picture Credits

Centers for Disease Control and Prevention, Public Health Image Library: 73, 151.

William H. Deaderick and Loyd Thompson. *The Endemic Diseases of the Southern States.* Philadelphia: W. B. Saunders, 1916: 9, 21, 64, 78.

H. Garman. *A Preliminary Study of Kentucky Localities in Which Pellagra Is Prevalent.* Lexington: Kentucky Agricultural Experiment Station of the State University, 1912: 53.

H. F. Harris. *Pellagra.* New York: Macmillan, 1919: 88.

Gail Jarrow: 12.

"Pellagracide and EZ-X-BA, Fraudulent Nostrums Sold as Cures of Pellagra," ***Journal of the American Medical Association***, March 2, 1912: 62, 63, back jacket.

C. H. Lavinder. *Pellagra: A Précis.* Washington, DC: Government Printing Office, 1908: 26.

C. H. Lavinder. *Pellagra: A Précis [Revised Edition].* Washington, DC: Government Printing Office, 1912: 29.

C. H. Lavinder, "The Prevalence and Geographic Distribution of Pellagra in the United States." ***Public Health Reports***, December 13, 1912: 39 (bottom).

Library of Congress, Prints & Photographs Division: HABS ALA, 49-MOUV, 1-C-1: 11; LC-USZ62-91717: 24 (left); LC-USZ62-77376: 24 (right); LC-USZ62-52347: 27; LC-USZ62-41743: 49 (bottom left); LC-USZ62-45055: 55; LC-USZ62-27886: 56; LC-USZ62-22339: 71; LC-USZ62-119508: 85; LC-USZ62-129558: 126; LC-USZ62-75847: 127; LC-DIG-ds-01294: 128 (top); LC-USZ62-53835: 128 (bottom); LC-USZ62-123851: 129; LC-USZ62-117125: 142; LC-USZ62-1854: 147; LC-USZ62-41744: 152; LC-USZ62-129482: 163. American National Red Cross Collection, LC-USZ62-101923: 132; LC-USZ62-101952: 137 (top); LC-USZ62-101920: 137 (bottom); LC-USZ62-101423: 138. George Grantham Bain Collection, LC-USZ62-21220: 52; LC-B2-2109-15: 70. Detroit Publishing Company Collection, LC-D418-8466: 150. Farm Security Administration-Office of War Information Photograph Collection, LC-USF33-006050-M4: 49 (right); LC-USZ62-130203: 141. National Child Labor Committee Collection, LC-USZ62-51053: 14; LC-USZ62-29085: 34 (top); LC-USZ62-52642: 34 (bottom); LC-USZ62-29080: 35 (top); LC-DIG-nclc-02772: 35 (bottom); LC-DIG-nclc-02573: 43; LC-USZ62-90632: 44 (top); LC-USZ62-55968: 44 (bottom); LC-

USZ62-63252: 46; LC-DIG-nclc-00438: 49 (top left); LC-DIG-nclc-00627: 95; LC-DIG-nclc-00599: 100; LC-USZ62-16426: 105; LC-USZ62-96800: 106 (top); LC-USZ62-29096: 107; LC-DIG-nclc-02596: 108; LC-DIG-nclc-00412: 110; LC-DIG-nclc-00414: 111. National Photo Company Collection, LC-USZ62-132069: 119; LC-F81-11532: 120. Work Projects Administration Poster Collection, LC-USZC2-5737: 143; LC-USZC2-1086: 145; LC-USZC2-5585: 154. World War I Posters Collection, LC-USZC4-9641: 117.

Armand Marie. *Pellagra*. Translated and adapted by C. H. Lavinder and J. W. Babcock. Columbia, SC: State Company, 1910: 4, 16, 20, 40, 50, 58, 83, 96.

National Conference on Pellagra Held Under Auspices of South Carolina State Board of Health, November 3 and 4, 1909. Transactions. Columbia, SC: State Company, 1910: 22.

National Library of Medicine, Images from the History of Medicine Collection: 18, 19, 38, 47, 61, 67, 72, 87, 91, 106 (bottom), 113, 116, 122, 125, 130, 134, 135, 136, 140.

George M. Niles. *Pellagra: An American Problem*. Philadelphia: W. B. Saunders, 1912: 32, 36.

Pellagra: A Report Upon 316 Cases of This Disease as Submitted by the Commission Appointed by the Tennessee State Board of Health. Nashville: Tennessee Pellagra Commission, 1911: 10, 59, 93.

Stewart R. Roberts. *Pellagra: History, Distribution, Diagnosis, Prognosis, Treatment, Etiology*. St. Louis: C. V. Mosby, 1912: front jacket, 6.

Courtesy of the **University of North Carolina at Chapel Hill**, Southern Historical Collection, Wilson Library: 69 (top and bottom), 76.

Courtesy of the **University of Wisconsin-Madison Archives**, Image #UW.UWArchives.031107as01.bib: 139.

Courtesy of the **Waring Historical Library**, Medical University of South Carolina: 15, 103.

Washington Post, August 30, 1910: 31.

Edward Jenner Wood. *A Treatise on Pellagra for the General Practitioner.* New York: D. Appleton, 1912: 81.

George A. Zeller, "The Spread of Pellagra Throughout the United States." *International Clinics*, 1911, vol. 1, series 21: 39 (top), 114.